COLLEGE
SECRETS
FOR *TEENS*

Money-Saving Ideas for the
Pre-College Years

COLLEGE SECRETS
FOR TEENS

Money-Saving Ideas for the
Pre-College Years

By Lynnette Khalfani Cox

Advantage World Press

Published by Advantage World Press
An Imprint of TheMoneyCoach.net, LLC
P.O. Box 1307
Mountainside, NJ 07092

Book Packaging: Earl Cox & Associates Literary Management

ISBN 10: 1-932450-12-2
ISBN 13: 978-1-932450-12-5

LCCN: 2014947295

Publishers Cataloging in Publication Data

Khalfani-Cox, Lynnette.

College secrets for teens : money-saving ideas for the pre-college years / by Lynnette Khalfani Cox. -- First edition. -- Mountainside, NJ : Advantage World Press, [2015]

pages ; cm.

ISBN: 1-932450-12-2 ; 978-1-932450-12-5
Includes index.
Summary: College costs often start several years before actual enrollment. Those costs include college exams, test preparation and tutors, pre-college programs and summer activities, campus tours and visits, and college application costs. In this book, you will learn all about pre-college expenses and how to minimize them. "College Secrets for Teens" and its companion book, "College Secrets", reveal the true costs of earning a college degree, including hidden higher-education expenses.--Publisher.

1. College preparation programs--United States--Costs. 2. Advanced placement programs (Education)--United States--Costs. 3. Campus visits--United States--Finance. 4. College entrance achievement tests--United States--Costs. 5. Universities and colleges--Entrance examinations--Costs. 6. College applications--United States--Costs. 7. College choice--United States. 8. College costs--United States. 9. High school students--United States--Finance, Personal. 10. College students--United States--Finance, Personal. 11. Saving and investment--United States. 12. Finance, Personal--United States. I. Title.

LB2342 .K472 2015   2014947295
378.3/80973--dc23   1501

Printed in the United States of America

First Edition: 2015

SPECIAL SALES

Advantage World Press books are available at special bulk purchase discounts to use for sales promotions, premiums, or educational purposes. For more information, write to Advantage World Press, Special Markets, P.O. Box 1307, Mountainside, NJ 07092, or e-mail info@themoneycoach.net.

*To my entire family, especially my dear husband, Earl.
Your love, discipline, organization and structure bring peace
and order to our ever-changing lives.*

*To some of the amazing teenagers and pre-teens I know
and love: Alexis, Andrea, Aziza, Dylan, Jakada, K.J., Lexi,
Madison, Nina, Parker, Sandra, Sydney, Tyler and Vinnie.*

*To all the young people out there determined to go to college, as
well as those students who are unsure of their future plans.*

*And to parents around the world who want the best for their
children, but are worried about paying for higher education.*

I wrote this book with all of you in my mind and heart.

OTHER BOOKS BY
LYNNETTE KHALFANI COX

College Secrets: How to Save Money, Cut College Costs and Graduate Debt Free

Zero Debt: The Ultimate Guide to Financial Freedom

Zero Debt for College Grads: From Student Loans to Financial Freedom

Perfect Credit: 7 Steps to a Great Credit Rating

Your First Home: The Smart Way to Get It and Keep It

The Money Coach's Guide to Your First Million

Investing Success: How to Conquer 30 Costly Mistakes & Multiply Your Wealth!

The Identity Theft Recovery Guide

Garage Sale Riches: The Millionaire Kids Club (Book 1)

Putting the 'Do' in Donate: The Millionaire Kids Club (Book 2)

Home Sweet Home: The Millionaire Kids Club (Book 3)

Penny Power: The Millionaire Kids Club (Book 4)

TABLE OF CONTENTS

$\mathscr{I}$NTRODUCTION

We all know that college is expensive. But what about the years *before* you — or your children — arrive at the college of your dreams?

Long before you or your offspring ever set foot on a college or university campus, you'll begin paying serious money toward earning that highly coveted college degree.

How much money? Well, that's the first eye-opener for a lot of parents and college-bound students.

College Secret:

Most middle-class families spend $5,000 to $10,000 or more on pre-college expenses and don't even realize it.

How is it possible that thousands of dollars in college expenses are incurred well before anyone even writes a check for tuition?

It's because, in reality, college costs start *at least a year* and often several years *before* a student actually enrolls in a particular four-year college or university.

Prior to college enrollment, a student typically encounters five categories of pre-college expenses. Those pre-college expenses are:

1. College Exams
    *   Standardized Admissions Tests
    *   College Credit or Placement Exams

2. Test Preparation and Tutors
3. Pre-College Programs and Summer Activities
4. Campus Tours and Visits
5. College Applications

At first glance, it may not seem like these pre-college expenses can put much of a dent in your budget. Indeed, some of you may not consider these true "college" expenses at all — since they happen *before* a college admits a student.

But omitting pre-college expenses from the equation is kidding yourself.

After all, real dollars are being spent on these items. So ignoring these costs or pretending they somehow "don't count" is engaging in financial fantasy.

To better illustrate my point about pre-college expenses, think for a moment about having a newborn child.

We all know that babies can be expensive. The cost of diapers, formula, and baby clothes — not to mention childcare for parents who need help — can all add up very quickly.

But do the costs associated with having a baby begin only once the child is born? Of course not.

Prior to the child's birth, there are a slew of expenses. For example, a pregnant mother must take prenatal pills, regularly visit her ob-gyn, and likely buy maternity clothes for her expanding body.

Parents must also prep for the child that is on the way. That could mean painting a bedroom, buying an infant car seat or purchasing a crib.

As any parent knows, bringing a child into the world is a huge life transition — one that takes time, and that costs money well *before* the child is even born.

Likewise, sending a student off to college is another major life transition — one that also takes time and requires *pre*-college funding to make the college-entrance transition possible.

Because of this reality, don't fool yourself into thinking that college costs happen only over the traditional four-years when a student is earning a degree.

When examined realistically, college costs should always be viewed from three different vantage points. There are:

1. *Pre-college* expenses to consider;
2. *Upfront* college costs you must be familiar with; and
3. *Hidden* college costs to take into account

College Secret:

Don't be hoodwinked: The *true* cost of college includes *pre-college* expenses, *upfront* college costs, as well as *hidden* "back end" fees.

In *College Secrets for Teens*, you'll learn all about pre-college expenses and how to minimize them.

In the flagship book in this series, called *College Secrets*, I tackle the huge litany of *upfront* college costs facing students — everything from tuition, fees, room and board to books, supplies, electronics and other required materials. I also cover the *hidden* costs of college, such as sneaky college surcharges known as "tuition differential," as well as a host of other expenses like penalty fees, "one-time" charges and service fees of all kinds.

High school juniors and seniors should definitely get a jump on the financial and academic planning process by checking out *College Secrets* so you know what to expect. If you're a high school freshman, sophomore — or even a teen in middle school — you may want to wait a bit before forging ahead with the other book in the *College Secrets* series. (Your parents may use it to help plan for you, though!)

Both books in this series cover completely different topics, but they each have the same goal: to help you cut educational costs so that finances don't hurt your chances of academic success.

A lack of money should never stop anyone from getting a good education. Unfortunately, that is often the reality for many post-secondary students, as financial challenges play a huge role in this country's abysmal college graduation rate.

Data from the U.S. Department of Education show that a mere 20% of students who start their higher education at two-year institutions finish their degrees in *three* years. Also, only about 40% of those attending four-year colleges and universities in the U.S. earn a degree in *six* years.

What's the main culprit behind these worrisome statistics? Six out of 10 college dropouts leave school simply because they can't afford it — or because they have to work so much to pay for college that they can't simultaneously juggle their jobs and academic responsibilities.

I don't think they're totally to blame for their plight, since college costs in America now exceed $20,000 annually at most public schools and $40,000 or more at the majority of private institutions. In fact, dozens of private colleges have sticker prices above $60,000 per year.

With the escalating cost of a four-year degree, it's little wonder that parents and students alike are so worried about higher education expenses.

Fortunately, you don't have to wind up buried in debt to receive a college education.

So if you're ready to jumpstart your future, let's start now with an in-depth look at all the *pre-college* experiences you may want or need. I'm going to show you how you can get them all — either free of charge, or at a price that you and your family can afford, no matter what your income or current financial standing.

CHAPTER 1

STANDARDIZED COLLEGE EXAMS AND TEST PREP

Students and parents alike are often stunned — and mortified — by the dizzying array of tests required in order to win acceptance into many four-year colleges.

You're probably familiar with the two heavyweights of the college testing world — the SAT and the ACT.

The SAT is a three-part exam that presently includes a Writing component, a Math section, and a Critical Reading portion. Test-takers can currently score a maximum of 800 points on each section, for a total possible maximum score of 2,400 on the SAT.

But effective in the spring of 2016, the SAT will return to its old 1,600-point system, in part, some people say, to better compete with its rival exam, the ACT.

The ACT is a four-part test that assesses a student's college readiness in four subjects: English, Math, Reading and Science. The ACT also offers an optional Writing test that requires test-takers to construct an essay. The highest possible ACT score is 36 points.

And just like the SAT, the ACT is in the midst of major changes.

The flagship ACT college-entrance exam will add what ACT officials call several key "enhancements" to the test starting in the spring of 2015. Among the changes: the ACT exam will gradually phase in computer-based testing. The ACT will also become more closely aligned with the Common Core state standards initiative.

Beyond the SAT and ACT, there's a litany of other exams that many college-bound students take, including:

- The PSAT (a pre-cursor to the SAT)
- The PLAN (the practice exam for the ACT)
- Advanced Placement or AP exams
- SAT IIs (also known as SAT Subject Tests)
- CLEP exams (the College Level Examination Program)
- The TOEFL (for students whose first language isn't English)
- Various state-specific exams required for high-school graduation

With the exception of state mandated examinations, all of these other tests cost money. Big bucks, in fact.

Students pay not only to *take* the above-mentioned tests. They also pay to *re-take* exams — sometimes over and over. And then many students pay yet again to have the tests *sent* to the colleges of their choice.

As a result, the college testing industry has mushroomed into a multi-billion dollar business.

More than 2 million students and their families spend some $9 billion a year on test preparation and tutoring, according to a report from IBISWorld.

The industry is comprised of test makers of all stripes, such as: ACT Inc., the American Council on Education, the Association of American Medical Colleges, the College Board, Educational Testing Service, the Graduate Management Admission Council, and the Law School Admission Council.

Additionally, there are the larger third-party test providers, including: Barron's Educational Series, Grockit Inc., Houghton Mifflin Harcourt, Huntington Learning Centers, Kaplan Inc., Knewton Inc., McGraw Hill Education, Manhattan Review, Pearson Education, The Princeton Review, and Veritas Prep.

By the way, these companies aren't just targeting high school students.

Every year, about 200,000 7th and 8th graders take the SAT or ACT, and the majority of them score as well as high school seniors who are four or five years older, according to a report called A Nation Deceived, about the need for acceleration of young people in education. The Acceleration Institute at the University of Iowa produced the report.

For the two most popular college entrance tests — the SAT and the ACT — here's what you can expect to pay.

SAT Registration Fees	
SAT Exam Registration	$51 per registration
SAT Basic Subject Test Registration	$24.50 per registration
SAT Language with Listening Test	$24 per test
All Other SAT Subject Tests	$13 per test

SAT Score Services Fees	
Additional Score Report Request	$11.25
Rush Order	$31
Scores By Phone	$15
Retrieval of Archived/Older Scores	$30.50
SAT Question and Answer Service	$18.50
SAT Student Answer Service	$13.50
Multiple Choice Score Verification	$55
Essay Score Verification	$55

SAT Additional Fees	
Register By Phone	$15
Change Fee	$27.50
Late Registration Fee	$27.50
Waitlist Fee	$45
International Processing Fees (required for test takers outside the U.S. and Canada)	$31, $35 or $50 based on region

Source: The College Board website; 2014 data

You'll also encounter a laundry list of fees for the ACT Exam.

ACT Registration Fees	
ACT (No Writing)	$36.50 per registration
ACT Plus Writing	$52.50 per registration

ACT Additional Registration Fees and Services	
Additional Score Reports	$12
Telephone Re-registration	$14
Late Fee Registration	$23
Standby Testing	$45
International Testing (outside U.S. and Canada)	$33
Test Date Change	$22
Test Information Release Service	$19
Multiple Choice Score Verification	$55
Essay Score Verification	$55

Source: The ACT website; 2014 data

I think you get the message that when it comes to college admissions testing, the costs can quickly add up.

Keep in mind too that among the nearly 1.7 million students that take the SAT each year and the roughly 1.8 million pupils who take the ACT, about one in four students re-takes these exams, further adding to college testing expenses.

All this testing is going on despite the fact that many educators question the merits of basing something as important as college admissions, in part, on a single day's test results.

Furthermore, parents and students alike are starting to complain — more loudly than ever — about the ever-growing cost of standardized tests.

In an op-ed piece in *The Wall Street Journal* in 2014, Benjamin Tonelli, then a senior at Garfield High School in Seattle, bemoaned the high price of pre-college testing.

"With college-admission deadlines quickly approaching, my debt to the College Board keeps growing," he wrote. "Two SAT tests, five subject tests and six Advanced Placement (AP) tests later, I am ready to report my scores through the College Board website to the 10 colleges to which I am applying. On top of the total $102 I paid to take the SAT, $114 for the subject tests, and $534 for the AP tests, the College Board now demands $11.25 for each electronic submission of the test scores to the schools on my list." (I'll help you with the math here. Tonelli paid $862.50 to the College Board).

"It seems odd that the College Board—a nonprofit whose CEO, David Coleman, was pulling in $750,000 as of 2012—cannot send a few numbers over the Internet for just a dollar or two, or maybe even free," Tonelli continued. "Instead, I am shoveling out another $100-plus just for electronic submissions, another contribution to the swelling pockets of the College Board (annual revenue in 2011-2012: more than $750 million)."

Tonelli was right about his numbers.

Although the College Board and ACT Inc. are both non-profit organizations, that doesn't mean this isn't a high-stakes business.

The College Board and ACT Inc. collectively rake in over a billion dollars annually.

According to the latest 990 form filed with the IRS by the College Board, it grossed a whopping $796 million in revenue in 2013. Meanwhile, ACT Inc. posted total annual revenue of $303 million in 2012, its most recent 990 form reveals.

So what can you do to reduce the amount of money you fork over for college tests?

There are four good solutions:

1. Consider "test optional" colleges
2. Get exam fee waivers
3. Use state vouchers
4. Pick the right test

Consider Test Optional Colleges

One way to bypass the expense (and the stress) of SAT and ACT testing is to simply go to a four-year school that doesn't require you to take those standardized exams.

Most people don't know that among degree-granting institutions, there are 2,774 four-year colleges and universities in America, including 672 public institutions and 2,102 private schools, according to the National Center for Education Statistics.

An even lesser-known fact is that you can get into *hundreds* of these colleges without ever taking either the SAT or ACT.

How is this possible?

All across the country, there are "test optional" or "test flexible" colleges and universities. These institutions de-emphasize college admissions tests — or often don't require them at all.

At more than 800 colleges and universities in the U.S., admissions officers are more than happy to admit you on the basis of factors other than test scores.

They place more value on your grades or overall grade-point average, class rank, college essays, school projects, extra-curricular activities, letters of recommendations and other elements of your college application.

In short, these "test flexible" schools realize that there are many ways to evaluate your candidacy beyond your ACT or SAT score.

College Secret:

More than 830 colleges and universities in America — about one-third of all nonprofit four-year institutions — do not require standardized college entrance exams.

These so-called "test optional" schools run the gamut — from small liberal arts colleges to big universities; private to public institutions; urban college campuses to schools in rural areas, and everything in between. And yes, there are *very good* schools among these campuses.

In fact, there are 140 test-flexible institutions ranked in the top tier of their respective categories by *U.S. News & World Report*.

Some of the prestigious liberal arts colleges with "test optional" or "test flexible" policies include:

- Bates College
- Bowdoin College
- Colby College
- Franklin and Marshall
- Hamilton College
- Middlebury College
- Muhlenberg College
- Smith College
- Wesleyan College

The list of nationally known universities that are test-optional is equally impressive and includes:

- American University
- Brandeis University
- New York University
- Texas A & M University
- University of Arizona
- University of Rochester
- University of Texas at Austin
- Wake Forest University
- Worcester Polytechnic Institute

Again, this is just a tiny sampling of some of the schools that fall into this category.

You can find the full list of colleges with flexible SAT and ACT test policies on the website maintained by the FairTest organization.

FairTest, also known as the National Center for Fair and Open Testing, says its mission is "to end the misuses and flaws of standardized testing and to ensure that evaluation of students, teachers and schools is fair, open, valid and educationally beneficial."

Even though FairTest keeps a comprehensive tally of "test flexible" schools, if you find a school you're interested in on the FairTest list, it's still important to go to that school's website for the finer points and details about its policies regarding testing.

That's because some schools may not require SAT or ACT scores for admissions, but still may use them for certain students, for placement purposes or to conduct research studies.

Also, note that if you're a student athlete applying to Patriot League schools and New England Small College Athletic Conference (NESCAC) schools (including so-called "Little Ivy" campuses like Williams, Amherst, and Middlebury), your ability to choose test optional is effectively squashed. That's because the athletic scholarship rules of those conferences require the colleges to report test scores.

What's Behind The Growth of Test Optional Colleges?

Some observers point to the overhaul of the SAT exam as an indication that the testing system is broken and that more colleges will likely abandon standardized test requirements in the future.

With all the hoopla, time, money and energy devoted to the world of college testing, you might be wondering why an ever-growing list of colleges would let students forgo taking admissions tests altogether.

It boils down to three main reasons, all of which influence many educators' and colleges' skepticism of standardized tests:

1. College admissions tests can be gamed
2. College admissions exams correlate very highly with family income, resulting in less diversity on campus
3. Tests like the SAT and ACT are <u>not</u> good predictors of college success

Critics of the SAT have long complained that the test is susceptible to coaching.

"If coaching doesn't work on the SAT, there are certainly a lot of deluded students and parents out there, many of whom are spending $1,000 or more for Kaplan and other test prep services," says Bob Schaeffer, Public Education Director for FairTest.

Calling the test nothing more than "a predictor of accumulated opportunity and family income," Schaeffer says: "The SATs are more strongly correlated with family income than they are with first year college grades, which is what they're supposed to predict."

Schaeffer's claims that expensive college prep activities play a big role in test scores seems to be borne out by data showing the high correlation between family income and scores.

As the chart below indicates, as you go up the ladder in household income scale, SAT test scores climb as well.

Observers point to this data as proof that kids from wealthier families — who can better afford test prep services, tutors and multiple rounds of college testing — have an unfair advantage when it comes to taking standardized tests.

But even if you put aside criticism about income inequality, the tests being unfair, or subject to gaming, perhaps the most damning criticism of college admissions tests is that they add little to no useful insights into the college admissions process.

According to a report from The National Association for College Admission Counseling, standardized tests simply are not good predictors of student performance in college.

In fact, when NACAC compared two groups of students — those who supplied tests scores for college admissions and students who didn't — the organization found no significant differences between the two groups as measured by graduation rates or cumulative GPA.

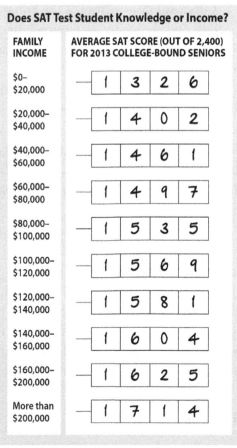

Does SAT Test Student Knowledge or Income?

FAMILY INCOME	AVERAGE SAT SCORE (OUT OF 2,400) FOR 2013 COLLEGE-BOUND SENIORS
$0–$20,000	1 3 2 6
$20,000–$40,000	1 4 0 2
$40,000–$60,000	1 4 6 1
$60,000–$80,000	1 4 9 7
$80,000–$100,000	1 5 3 5
$100,000–$120,000	1 5 6 9
$120,000–$140,000	1 5 8 1
$140,000–$160,000	1 6 0 4
$160,000–$200,000	1 6 2 5
More than $200,000	1 7 1 4

Source: The College Board

And NACAC's study didn't represent a brief snapshot of just a handful of students.

On the contrary, that study examined nearly 123,000 students at 33 different public and private institutions over an eight-year period.

Furthermore, the study found that a student's high school GPA was a far more accurate determinant of college success than test scores.

High school GPAs correlated highly with college GPAs, regardless of SAT or ACT scores. In effect, students who had low high school GPAs but high SAT or ACT scores typically fared poorly in college. But students with strong high school GPAs and low SAT or ACT scores nonetheless performed well in college.

"This data is the hard evidence that admissions offices need to change their policies requiring standardized tests," says Schaeffer.

Other studies — from Wake Forest, the University of California, Bates College and elsewhere — reinforce the NACAC's findings.

All of this explains, in part, the growth behind the test optional movement among colleges.

Even with the new SAT to be launched in 2016, standardized testing won't change much, Schaeffer says.

"There's no evidence that the test will be a better predictor of college success, or that it will be any more fair to help level the playing field," among students of various economic backgrounds, Schaeffer says. "So we don't think the new SAT is going to have any impact at all on the pace of test-optional growth."

But does that mean test scores don't matter? Certainly not. In fact, when it comes to getting money from a college, some college experts say test scores matter more than grades.

"It's pretty simple," Ian Welham, a college-funding specialist with Complete College Planning Solutions in Springfield, NJ, once told Forbes magazine. "If you want more money, increase your test scores. Regardless of what the college tour guide or the glitzy brochure says, the kid with the 800 in math will get the money over the kid with straight A's."

To Test or Not To Test

For better or worse, however, college testing remains a huge part of the admissions landscape for high school students, and this reality will probably continue for the foreseeable future. In fact, the roadway to college now involves testing and evaluations of 7- and 8-year olds.

Yes, you read that right. College testing now targets students as young as *seven years old!*

In April 2014, the ACT organization (in partnership with Pearson) launched ACT Aspire, which is billed as a next-generation college and career readiness system that tests students from *3rd grade* through 10th grade.

This new ACT testing program is administered online only and features five subject areas: English, reading, writing, math and science.

In an announcement marking the 2014 rollout of ACT Aspire to 66,000 students in 33 states, Kevin Howell, the CEO of ACT Aspire said: "Our program is a connected, longitudinal progression from grade 3 through early high school that anchors with the ACT exam. And, our program will be predictive as student data is measured over time."

"Using decades of research gained from the administration of the ACT, ACT Aspire identifies where a student stands at the time of testing, and suggests a predictive trajectory of how that student is likely to progress across the grades," Howell added.

That's not all. Equally important changes have already impacted other ACT test offerings.

In years past, the ACT organization offered a test called ACT Explore, which was for 8th graders. ACT also had the ACT Plan — an exam for 10th graders that served as a precursor to the actual ACT. As of mid-June 2014, however, ACT officials did away with test administration and scoring for the Explore and PLAN exams.

Beginning with the 2014-2015 academic term, ACT Aspire replaced ACT Explore and ACT Plan as ACT's sole college readiness testing system.

By aggressively expanding its assessment options, and offering a new integrated test program that analyzes student learning as early as third grade, the ACT is essentially trying to show the link between college preparedness and achievement of certain benchmarks (namely, Common Core standards) in the lower grades.

That approach strikes some people as unfair and unwise; especially critics who hate the Common Core or those who abhor testing in general.

These critics ask: *Are we prepared to believe that a 10-year-old 5th grader who hasn't met various academic milestones is destined to have a poor ACT performance as an 11th or 12 grader?*

ACT officials respond to such criticism by saying that early testing can give a warning signal to educators and parents, allowing time for intervention and more instruction to help a student's academic deficiencies. But critics worry whether teachers may start (consciously or unconsciously) to write off some students deemed to be poor performers who are not likely to improve.

Critics also say earlier, additional testing places undue testing stress on students –not to mention that it creates even more anxiety for parents who already fret about the college admissions process.

But the truth of the matter is that ACT Inc. is far from alone it its approach.

Competing early-testing offerings are underway from several ACT competitors, including the Smarter Balanced Consortium. The Consortium is a collaboration of 22 states led by educators, researchers and policy makers. The Consortium is developing its own system of assessments for English language arts and math for students in grades 3 through 11. Like the ACT's Aspire suite of tests, the Consortium's assessments align with the Common Core standards.

There's also PARCC, or the Partnership for Assessment of Readiness for College and Careers, which lines up with the Common Core as well.

PARCC is a comprised of educators and policymakers in various states who are working together to develop a set of computer-based tests for students in *kindergarten* through 12th grade. The tests cover Mathematics and English Language Arts/Literacy. The PARCC assessments launch in 16 states plus the District of Columbia during the 2014-15 school year.

All three models — the ACT Aspire, the SBAC assessment system, and PARCC — are designed to test students *early* and *annually*, and measure whether those youth are on track to graduate from high school equipped for success in college and/or in their careers.

Whether or not all this testing and evaluation at lower and lower grade levels proves accurate — or is even a good idea — remains to be seen.

But one thing is certain: an ironic pattern is emerging in the realm of standardized tests. More and more testing is being required of students at ever-younger ages, and at the same time, fewer and fewer colleges and universities are requiring mandatory testing for first-year applicants.

College Secret:

Standardized testing is being required *more* frequently for elementary and middle school pupils, but *less* frequently for high school students going to college.

Despite this paradox, it's probably a good bet that increasing numbers of post-secondary schools will keep moving away from a heavy reliance on standardized tests, even if only as a matter of best practice.

For example, NACAC's "Statement of Principles of Good Practice" states that colleges and universities should "not use minimum test scores as the sole criterion for admission, advising, or for the awarding of financial aid."

This sentiment is echoed by the testing practices developed by other educational groups, including the American Educational Research Association, the American Psychological Association and the National Council on Measurement in Education.

So the bottom line is this: although testing is being ratcheted up for ever-younger students, by the time they get older, thanks to the test optional movement, students may not have to buy (literally and figuratively) into the whole college testing craze.

Get Exam Fee Waivers

For now, if you're seeking admission to schools that do require standardized tests, getting fee waivers is a practical way to eliminate various costs for these exams.

Here's what you need to know about SAT and ACT fee waivers.

SAT Fee Waiver Eligibility

According to the College Board, if you are a U.S. citizen or an American citizen residing outside the country, you qualify for an SAT fee waiver if you fall into any of the following categories:

- You are enrolled in or eligible to participate in the federal Free and Reduced Price Lunch program
- Your annual family income falls within the Income Eligibility Guidelines set by the USDA Food and Nutrition Service (see income chart below)
- You are enrolled in a federal, state, or local program that aids students from low-income families (examples include Federal TRIO programs like Upward Bound, Talent Search and Student Support Services)
- Your family receives public assistance (such as food stamps)
- You live in federally subsidized public housing, a foster home, or are homeless
- You are a ward of the state or an orphan

Number of Members In Household (including Head of Household)	Total Annual Income (in prior calendar year)
1	$21,590
2	$29,101
3	$36,612
4	$44,123
5	$51,634
6	$59,145

Household size is considered the number of household members, plus the filer on the family's current tax statement. Also, a student in foster care is considered a household size of one person.

And what if you have more than six family members in your household?

You take the annual allowance for six members, which was $59,145 in 2014-2015, and then add $7,511 for each additional member. If you're reading this book after June 30, 2015, be sure to look up the most recent income caps, as the government usually increases these figures by a few hundred dollars yearly.

SAT fee waivers are only available to students in 9th, 10th, 11th and 12th grades. Sorry: any of you 7th and 8th graders taking the SAT can't get fee waivers.

Students taking the SAT can use their fee waivers in either their junior or senior years of high school. Students taking the SAT Subject Tests can use fee waivers in their freshman, sophomore, junior or senior years.

The College Board recently provided $72 million in fee waivers and discounts to students. That's great. But I estimate that based on income and other eligibility factors cited above, millions of the nation's 20 million public and private high school students can qualify for an SAT fee waiver. However, only a fraction of those students request them.

For example, there are 31 million elementary and secondary school students getting free and reduced lunch in the United States. But since this lunch aid initiative is an opt-in program at most schools, researchers believe that high school students — who may feel embarrassed about getting free lunch — are greatly under-represented in school lunch program enrollment. These students (and likely their parents) probably have no idea that taking part in a free lunch program at school could also help them qualify for important exam fee waivers that will promote their college eligibility.

Also, about 44 million Americans get SNAP benefits, or food stamps, including 20 million youth. Not all of these are high school students, of course. Once these young people do enter 9th grade, though, if their families are still receiving public benefits, they'd be wise to seek fee waivers for their college entrance exams.

College Secret:

SAT fee waivers, which let certain students take the SAT exam free of charge, are vastly under utilized. These waivers could save families millions of dollars annually.

There's a final note of importance about SAT fee waivers. The College Board has *no cap* on fee waivers. This means the organization will provide fee waivers to an *unlimited* number of students who need assistance. The College Board's goal in this regard is very simple and admirable: to aid any and all students for whom the cost of an exam would be a barrier to college entry.

ACT Fee Waiver Eligibility

For students from low-income households, qualification for a fee waiver for the ACT Exam has similar requirements to the SAT exam waiver's requirements.

According to the ACT website, to be eligible for an exam waiver you must meet all of the following requirements:

1. Be currently enrolled in high school in the 11th or 12th grade.
2. Be either a United States citizen or testing in the U. S., U.S. territories, or Puerto Rico.
3. Satisfy one or more indicators of economic need listed on the ACT Fee Waiver form.

The ACT's "indicators of economic need" are identical to the financial conditions listed for an SAT fee waiver.

For more information about test waivers, see the College Board and ACT websites. The specific links that will help are: SAT.org/fee-waivers and ACTStudent.org/faq/feewaiver.html.

How to Obtain a Test Fee Waiver

Even though fee waivers can let you take the SAT or ACT exams free of charge, the organizations that administer those exams don't give you the waivers directly.

Instead, you must go to your high school counselor and let him or her know that you need a waiver. For those in foster care, an agency official will need to give you the waiver.

Because school and agency officials must verify your financial hardship, it's best to get them involved as soon as possible.

Don't be afraid, ashamed — or even too proud — to request a test waiver if you know you meet the qualification guidelines, or if paying for a college test would be a financial hardship.

Home-schooled students must provide proof of eligibility (like tax records, public assistance records or confirmation of enrollment in an aid program) to a local high school counselor.

When a school counselor determines that you are eligible, you can receive up to four SAT fee waiver cards. Those cards will allow you to take the SAT exam twice, and have two SAT Subject Test registrations.

To use your fee waiver to actually register for the SAT exam, you simply mail your registration or register online at sat.org/register.

On the website, you'll have to supply various pieces of information from your fee waiver card, including the 12-digit code on your fee waiver, your high school counselor's name, and the eligibility criteria you meet.

For the ACT, you'll get a fee waiver that has a "serial code" that you use to take the test at no charge.

The Benefits of Fee Waivers

One of the best things about SAT fee waivers is that they cover far more than just the testing fees.

Regardless of whether you're taking the SAT (also called the SAT I) or SAT Subject Tests (sometimes called SAT IIs), your fee waiver will cover:

- The registration fee for the SAT or SAT Subject Tests (with the latter, you can take up to three individual SAT Subject Tests during a single test day)
- Four additional score reports (you can order these at no charge at any time after registering for the test(s) — even after you have seen your scores.
- Question-and-Answer Service or Student Answer Service, if ordered at the time of registration. (For the SAT, these services give you feedback about various test questions — including whether they were easy, moderate or difficult — and how you answered each
- Up to four Request for Waiver of College Application Fee forms
- A $40 discount off the regular price of The Official SAT Online Course when you register online using a fee waiver
- Any fees associated with registering internationally
- Late registrations (this is a new benefit which started in 2014-2015)

As you can see, SAT fee waivers can help you keep a lot of cash in your pocket and help you prepare for college. Getting up to four waivers on college application forms is an especially good money-saver because college application fees can run as much as $75 to $90 each.

If you are eligible for an ACT waiver, you can use a maximum of two separate fee waivers. Once you register, the waiver is considered use — regardless of whether you actually take the test on the date you chose.

ACT fee waivers only cover the basic registration fee, plus scores for up to four college choices (if you provide valid codes when you register). ACT waivers can't be used to pay for late fees, changes to your test date or test center, standby fees or any other services.

Likewise, one downside with SAT waivers is that you can't use them for all the fees charged by the College Board.

For instance, SAT waivers aren't good for waitlist requests or change fees. Also, your fee-waiver code is good for only one registration.

So if you register with an SAT fee waiver and then you miss the test day for any reason, you won't be able to re-register with the identical fee-waiver code. At that point, you'll have to call or go online and pay a change fee to transfer your registration to another test date.

For some high school students, it may be a bit early to consider what you'll do after earning a four-year degree. But others may already know that getting an advanced degree is in their future. If that's the case, know that if you're interested in pursuing graduates studies, there are fee waivers available for low-income students who must take the GRE, GMAT, LSAT or MCAT.

These are the tests you take to gain entrance into graduate school, business school, law school and medical school, respectively. Since various testing boards run each exam, the eligibility standards and application process for fee waivers vary. So consult each agency's website for the latest details on how you can reduce or eliminate graduate exam fees.

Use State Vouchers

Another way to escape the costs associated with taking the ACT or SAT is to take a test free of charge if your state offers vouchers for a college entrance exam.

Back in 2001, the No Child Left Behind Act mandated that high schools test students in math, science and reading. As a result of that law, several states adopted the ACT as an achievement exam. Since the ACT is curriculum-based, states recognized that the test could fulfill the requirements imposed by No Child Left Behind.

The good financial news in all of this — at least for students and their families — was that states forked over the money to pay for this mandatory testing of high school kids. The process was fairly easy, too. Students simply received vouchers from their high school counselors.

Fast-forward to 2014 and 13 states were administering the ACT test statewide.

Among these regions, Colorado, Hawaii, Illinois, Kentucky, Louisiana, Michigan, Montana, North Carolina, North Dakota, Tennessee, Utah and Wyoming require students to take the test. The state of Arkansas pays for the ACT exam if districts want to offer it.

Minnesota, Mississippi, Missouri, and Wisconsin are also expected to start giving the ACT to high school students in their respective territories in 2015, pushing the total number of states contracted to offer ACT testing to 17.

So if you live in any of these states, you get to take the ACT free of charge — a nice savings considering that for the Spring 2015 exam, the ACT is going up a buck to a cost of $37.50 for the basic test. It will still cost an extra $16 for the Writing add-on, meaning the 2015 price is $53.50 for the ACT Plus Writing.

ACT vouchers cover only the regular registration fees for the ACT without writing, including reports to a student's high school and up to four colleges. But state vouchers don't cover late fees, test date or location changes, standby fees and other charges. Also, if you want to take the ACT Plus Writing, you have to pay the extra $16 fee.

Get more info on the ACT voucher and sign-up process online at: http://www.actstudent.org/regist/voucher.html

As for the SAT, that exam is offered at no cost to students in three states: Delaware, Idaho and Maine. So students in those areas can save $52 a pop by getting vouchers from their high school counselors too.

States that pay for students to sit for the ACT or SAT exam are doing so in a bid to integrate college admissions tests into state systems, thereby reducing the amount of overall testing students must undergo.

Even if you don't live in one of the above-mentioned states, it's a good idea to keep tabs on this issue. Both the ACT and the College Board will no doubt add to their list of state contracts for college testing.

Pick the Right Test

A fourth and final strategy to lower testing costs is to focus exclusively on one test, either the SAT or the ACT. Don't take both. At least this way you potentially cut your college testing expenses in half — if not more.

But this strategy has to be done the right way in order to be effective.

To pick the right test, and optimize your chance of a high score, you should play to your academic strengths. To do this, you have to know your own curricular and testing strengths and weaknesses, and consider how each college entrance exam is constructed.

Don't just take one exam over another because it seems to be a popular choice at your school or because you've heard one test is "easier" than the other.

Without a strong sense of your academic and testing capabilities, you'll be forced to do what a lot of students do — and that is take *both* tests and then go with the test that produces the higher score.

At first glance, that approach may seem logical. But it totally defeats the purpose of trying to cut down on your test costs and your overall pre-college expenses. It's also arguably not the best or most efficient use of a student's time, because of the attendant prep work that needs to precede exam day.

Which Test is Most Popular?

Historically, the SAT has been more popular in the Northeast as well as the West Coast and the Washington DC metro area. The SAT's heavy East Coast appeal may have initially been attributable to two circumstances: first the SAT was launched in 1926 at Princeton University, which is in New Jersey. Also, the Northeast is home to multiple clusters of elite schools spanning a range of desirable cities, including Boston, New York and Philadelphia.

But some 30-plus years after the launch of the SAT, the ACT was created in 1959.

Year after year, the ACT grew in usage and the by early 2000s it started making significant headway — especially in the South, as well as at schools in Middle America.

These days the ACT has overtaken the SAT in popularity.

In 2012, the ACT edged the SAT in sheer numbers for the first time, when 1,666,017 students took the ACT, and about 1,664,479 students took the SAT.

In 2013, the ACT again topped the SAT, with some 1.8 million students opting for the ACT and nearly 1.7 million taking the SAT.

So which test is right for you?

Core Differences Between the ACT and SAT Exams

The SAT and ACT are fundamentally different — and if you have to sit for a multi-hour test, you might as well strategically use those tests' differences to your advantage.

As previously mentioned, the ACT contains four long sections: English, Reading, Math, and Science. There's also an optional writing section.

By comparison, the SAT has 10 smaller sections covering Critical Reading, Writing, Math and an Essay.

Remember, though, that in the year 2016 the College Board will drop the SAT's essay requirement and make it optional. The revised math section will also give students more time: 80 minutes to finish 60 questions on the new SAT test.

Also, a revised ACT exam debuts in the spring of 2015, with several key changes: among them, students will get a new STEM score, which is a combination of their scores in math and science. For students who take the optional writing portion of the ACT, they'll receive a new English/Language Arts score, which will be calculated by adding up their English, reading and writing scores.

In the meantime, think about your ability to concentrate and your test-taking prowess. Are you able to stay focused for long periods of time and to grasp material in big chunks? If so, the ACT could play to such skills. On the other hand, if you find it easy to jump from topic to topic, and prefer to answer questions in smaller sections, the SAT might be preferable.

There are many other points to consider.

Some students feel that the math portion of the ACT is more challenging, since that exam has more advanced concepts, like trigonometry. Because the ACT has an entire section dealing with science, those who are good in science also may favor the ACT.

Students who love reading, writing and vocabulary should strongly consider the SAT since those areas dominate the test.

If you're a slow to moderate-paced reader, you may fare better on the SAT as well.

That's because the SAT gives students more time: 70 minutes to complete 67 reading questions, and 35 minutes to answer 49 writing questions.

Experts say you generally have to be faster taking the ACT, since more speed is required to finish the ACT exam's 75 English questions in just 45 minutes, along with 40 reading questions in 35 minutes.

Consider also *how* the test will be administered. Will you use good old-fashioned paper and pencil, or will you be taking a digital test?

If you don't know which is more comfortable for you, try taking sample tests on your own to see which method makes you feel more confident.

Tech-savvy students may prefer online tests. But those who aren't quite comfortable using digital technology should know that well before taking a test. You don't want computer fears or a lack of knowledge about testing online to fray your nerves on test day.

Finally, don't lose any sleep thinking that colleges have a preference for one test or another.

"We don't care if students submit the SAT or the ACT," says Karen Richardson, Associate Director of Admissions at Tufts University. "We take either the SAT and two subject tests or the ACT with Writing."

Money-Saving Test Prep Advice

If you ultimately find that you need to take a college entrance exam to get into the school of your choice or to make yourself more competitive, you'll no doubt want to study to properly prepare for the test you'll be taking.

That's why college test prep is big business in America.

Scores of anxious parents want to give their kids a competitive edge in the college admissions process. As a result, some families are willing to spend many hundreds or even many thousands of dollars on test prep services.

SAT prep classes from Kaplan Test Prep and Princeton Review can cost more than $1,000. And one-on-one SAT and ACT coaching from private tutors typically ranges from about $50 to $300 an hour, depending on where in the country you live.

But paying such high fees isn't necessary. And while wealthy families may be able to better afford high-cost test prep, this option is generally out of the question for most low-income and even many middle-income families.

Thankfully, there are clear alternatives to paying for pricey college test preparation services. Here are some no-cost solutions:

1. Tap free online tutorials
2. Use paper-based sample tests
3. Enroll in a school-based test prep class
4. Form study groups
5. Create an independent self-study plan

The Best Free Online Tutorials

A number of companies and organizations provide free online college test prep for students, starting with the makers of the SAT and ACT, both of which offer a wealth of complimentary testing materials and exam tips via their websites.

Here are some other complimentary college entrance exam resources.

Number2.com is a web site that provides free tutorials, practice questions, and vocabulary drills for students prepping for the SAT, ACT and even the GRE (the Graduate Records Examination). Like several online players in this space, Number2.com offers a "word of the day" to help build a student's vocabulary.

But there are two other unique aspects of this site worth knowing about.

First, the ACT and SAT test prep courses offered by Number2.com adapt to a student's personal skill level — raising the bar for students by steadily challenging them, and building their knowledge and skills as they continually learn more.

Second, the Number2.com site features an interactive "coaching" section for parents, educators or counselors. This coaching platform allows a third-party, such as a parent, to monitor a student's progress by viewing real-time reports. The reports summarize all kinds of data about the student's online habits, including time spent online studying at Number2. com, questions answered, and even difficult words that a student may have missed in the vocabulary section.

Parents and teachers can sign up as "coaches" on Number2.com. Alternatively, students can nominate others as coaches, and then those adults can confirm their willingness to act as mentors, and track the student's study progression.

I signed up as a coach on Number2.com for my oldest daughter and liked the site a lot. I also appreciated that Number2.com is a very clean, advertising-free website that doesn't solicit money from students or parents and doesn't pitch any products or services. Instead, Number2.com earns revenue from sponsorships and licensing.

Test Prep Review is another complimentary site where students can score everything from online tests to daily SAT or ACT video lessons. But be forewarned: one downside of this site is that it does prominently feature products for sale — like ACT flashcards and SAT Study Guides. If you can cut through those advertising pitches and stick to the material found in the "Free Practice Test" links on the left column of the site, you'll find lots of good information.

Even Kaplan, which most people think of as a paid test prep service, offers several no-cost online options for students. For example, Kaplan provides free Internet-based SAT, ACT and PSAT practice tests and information sessions all year long. One of Kaplan's online sessions is dubbed: *5 Most Missed SAT Questions & 5 Must-Know Strategies to Raise Your Score.* Another is called *Free ACT Online Practice Test + Score Review.* You can search for specific dates and enroll in these free online tutorials from Kaplan at http://Kaptest.com/hsevents.

One of the other best-known and most well-respected online learning platforms in the marketplace today is Khan Academy, the education-focused non-profit company that in early 2014 announced a partnership with the College Board to offer free SAT test prep to any student that wants it.

Under the arrangement, Khan Academy will provide its instructional videos, Web-based practice problems, online tests, and other interactive tools to help students improve SAT performance.

The new partnership, according to College Board President David Coleman, was created in large part to level the playing field for those who can't afford expensive college test prep.

"The College Board cannot stand by while some test-prep providers intimidate parents at all levels of income into the belief that the only way to secure their child's success is to pay for costly test preparation and coaching," Coleman said in announcing the joint venture with Khan Academy. "It's time to shake things up."

As part of that shake-up, students can go to the Khan Academy website to access hundreds of previously unreleased questions from past SAT exams.

In the spring of 2015 — one year before the new, re-designed SAT is slated to debut in 2016 — Khan Academy's site will also roll out additional, College Board-branded materials and tools, including adaptive and game-based online instruction.

Test prep for the ACT is abundant as well. But some people say the test prep frenzy is far more pronounced around the SAT.

"There's much less evidence about coaching for the ACT," Schaeffer, the FairTest expert, notes.

One possible reason, some say, is that the ACT was developed to measure what students should have already learned in high school. As a result, some students may not feel the need to prep as much for that exam.

By the way, for any readers wondering whether online test prep and online education is useful or fruitful, the answer is a resounding yes.

There are two big benefits to using free online programs. Not only are students cutting costs, but they are also setting themselves up for academic success and lifelong learning.

Research from UCLA shows that students who engage in independent learning — just learning something on their own online rather than having to do it for a class — are better lifelong learners.

"Students who chose to independently use online instructional websites are also more likely to exhibit behaviors and traits associated with academic success and lifelong learning," UCLA researchers noted.

Additionally, online education seems to be the wave of the future at the collegiate level, and this trend is occurring both in the U.S. and internationally. So it may benefit high school students to get used to this reality now.

Among colleges, universities and other higher education providers, there is a boom in so-called "open educational resources." This includes a variety of online sites offering free education such as MIT OpenCourseWare, and Massive Open Online Courses (MOOCs) via such places as Coursera, edX, and Udacity.

Paper-Based Sample Tests

Another way to effectively prep for college exams — without shelling out big bucks — is to use free, paper-based sample tests.

You can find these from the test makers themselves, such as ACT Inc. or the College Board, as well as a number of other places. Some starting points: sample tests in library books can be photocopied; current and/or previous years' practice exams can be obtained from high school counselors; and teachers may have extra copies of older college tests too. All can be helpful learning tools.

Of course, there's also a world of information at your fingertips via the Web.

Just use Google, Yahoo! or Bing to do an online search of a phrase like "free ACT practice exam" or "free SAT practice test." It will turn up a large number of sites where you can find tests. When you locate a free college exam, just print it out and off you go.

College-oriented sites, such as College Confidential, are often very helpful too in tracking down actual printed college tests. Their message boards frequently post online links to past college entrance exams that can be used for study purposes.

School-Based Test Prep

Various high schools across the country offer college test prep classes as part of their curriculum. If this is the case at your school, taking such a course gives you an instant free way to bone up on the SAT or ACT exam.

Sometimes, students or parents may not even know that such courses exist in their school. So ask a counselor.

If you find out that your school doesn't offer a class, it's worth lobbying for one in the future — especially if you have younger siblings will be attending the same high school and could benefit from a class down the road.

And even if your school lacks an SAT or ACT prep course, that doesn't prohibit you from nicely asking a good Math or English teacher for one-on-one help during lunch or office hours.

Form Study Groups

Forming a study group is probably one of the most under-utilized techniques for students prepping for standardized college tests. But think about the brilliance of this strategy and how effective it could be.

You assemble a small group of students, all of whom have to take the SAT or ACT, and you let them learn together and help one another. Some students may opt to pair up with their opposites. For example, a student who is very strong in language arts might team up with another pupil who has stellar math skills.

In some cases, however, it may not even matter whether students have similar or disparate abilities or interests. The idea is to get a group going to increase the likelihood that regular, consistent studying will actually take place.

It's much easier for a student to blow off a study session if he or she is working solo. But being in a group means greater accountability. It can also be helpful for students to bounce questions, information and test-taking strategies off one another.

Best of all: the study group is free, yet it offers the potential for a dynamic, high-collaboration learning environment.

And remember: the ability to get along in a group is an important lifelong skill that goes far beyond college testing and college prep. Once students get into the real world, they'll have to often work in teams in the workforce.

Create an Independent Study Plan

For diligent students who are ambitious and focused, or for those who would stick to a study plan if prodded by mom or dad, an independent study plan is another viable, free test prep method.

In preparing for the PSAT/National Merit exam and the SAT, my daughter, Aziza, who is a very good student, used four of the strategies previously mentioned, with the exception of taking an SAT prep course for a semester or a year in school. (And one was, in fact, offered at her school).

But for just over three months, she frequented Khan Academy and other online sites almost daily. She took numerous paper tests and got accustomed to bubbling in answers quickly and working under tight testing deadlines.

She also had a study partner — yours truly! — the entire time. We spent many weekends studying and testing together. And although it was grueling (more for *me* than for *her*), I like to think that I was a big help to my daughter in all areas related to reading and writing.

I can say with certainty that I was of absolutely no substantive use at all on the math sections, since I didn't recall even half of the math on those tests! Still, that didn't stop me from yelling "Start!" or "Stop!" to help my daughter stick to the time limits on the tests. I also insisted that she not "veg out" Friday nights and instead use that time wisely to study. (Can you say *Tiger Mom?*)

We created an independent study plan for her college testing efforts by blocking off time in her schedule to devote solely to studying. That was no small challenge, considering her regular studies, extracurricular activities, drama performances and more. And like most growing teenagers, she also found time for sleep (lots of it in my opinion; not enough in her opinion).

In the end, my daughter did extremely well on the October 2013 PSAT, scoring a 225, and earning a place as a 2015 National Merit Scholarship Semifinalist from the state of New Jersey.

My daughter's strong PSAT performance convinced me that she was a teen who didn't need ultra lengthy — or ridiculously expensive — college test prep.

When she took the SAT in January 2014, she scored a 2,130. That's a very good score, but she wanted to aim higher. "I want a perfect score, Mom," she told me. So she signed up to re-take the SAT in June 2014. Meantime, she took three SAT II exams — in French, Literature and Math 2 — in May 2014.

To prepare her for the SAT the second time, we used the exact same free college test prep strategies that we employed for the PSAT: mainly her studying and reviewing, and me testing her again and again. She did three practice tests in preparation for her second SAT sitting since we believe in the old adage: "practice makes perfect."

But this time around, I also spent exactly $210 for additional test prep. Here's where the money went.

I bought *The Official SAT Study Guide* for $21.99, and the second edition of *The Official Study Guide for All SAT Study Tests* for $22.99, from the College Board. Knowing that my daughter is a bookworm, who actually enjoys learning via books, I figured those updated guides would be helpful for her SAT reviews — and invaluable as additional sources of sample tests. I further knew that my son could use these books upon entering high school in the fall of 2014.

Besides the books, I also signed my daughter up for a Weekend SAT Boot Camp conducted by a company called Catalyst Prep. The cost: $165.

After checking out the Catalyst program online, we collectively decided it would be worth the investment, which, for us, was modest. When she attended the boot camp, which was held at her high school, she came home thrilled about having attended.

My daughter actually told me: "This was probably the single best test prep I could have ever taken." Among many things, she said one key advantage of the crash course was learning a variety of rules, tips and tricks to use in tackling both the Verbal and Math sections of the SAT. Interestingly, the Catalyst boot camp included two diagnostic exams that my daughter also took. Based on the results of those diagnostic assessments, the company predicted her new SAT score would be 2,200, a 70-point improvement over her original score. I thought: "We'll see."

In early July 2014, we learned her scores and they were better than expected — at least higher than Catalyst forecast: 2,230; a 100-point increase.

So what did the trick? Was it our constant studying and testing efforts, the Catalyst boot camp, a combination of these factors — or something else altogether? We'll never really know. But I do know that both repeated testing and strategic prep work bolstered my daughter's confidence and helped her perform at her best when it counted most.

My daughter is obviously just one student, and every student is different. But the moral of this whole story is: Please don't think you have to spend a ton of money on college test prep. In most cases, it's simply not necessary.

In fact, some studies have shown that test prep doesn't boost college entrance scores anywhere near as much as test prep marketers would have you believe. One survey found that the average score improvement after test prep was just 30 points.

College Secret:

Paying for an expensive test prep course may or may not pay off. Some research suggests that test scores only improve modestly after prep sessions.

Personally, I think that all forms of serious test prep — whether free or paid — will be beneficial to students. The question is: to what extent? And if you're paying for test prep, is it worth the cost? Frankly, I believe that many, many students can forgo expensive paid college test prep altogether and still do very well.

No matter where you land on the issue of using paid vs. free test prep, I have to say that I think that it's practically a sin to send your kid into taking such an important test completely cold, *with no prep whatsoever*. That's doing him or her a disservice.

At the very least, a teenager should know what type of material will be on a test, how long the overall test is and how much time is allotted to each section, whether guessing is penalized, what kind of questions to expect, and so on. Even taking just *one* sample test before the real test can help immensely.

But parents, you know your kids. And students, you know yourselves.

So do yourselves a favor. Start by picking the best *free* college test prep strategy that will work for you. Only after doing that should you consider supplementing those efforts — if you want — with paid, preferably affordable test prep options.

CHAPTER 2

*A*CADEMIC *E*NRICHMENT AND *C*OLLEGE *L*EVEL *C*LASSES

In general, there are four different ways to experience some of the academic (and sometimes social) aspects of college while you're still in high school. It boils down to:

- Pre-College Summer Programs
- Early Entrance Programs
- Early College High Schools; and
- College-Level Classes

Chapters 3 through 5 will deal with pre-college summer programs in detail. But first, here is a brief overview of each pre-college academic enrichment option.

A Primer on Pre-College Summer Programs

One type of pre-college offering is an academic or enrichment program provided right on a college or university campus. These are offered in two ways: directly from colleges and universities, or by third-party marketers who create these programs in collaboration with host college campuses. Both offerings are typically summer pre-college programs. Some are free; others range from low-cost (anywhere from $50 up to $500 a week) to moderately priced (around $500 to $1,000 weekly) to expensive (roughly $1,000 to $2,500 or more per week).

What can you expect at a typical campus-based, pre-college summer program?

It largely depends on the program. Some summer pre-college programs are heavy on academics and studying — to the point where kids earn college credit (usually 3 to 6 credits) for their efforts.

Others focus on social interaction, leisure activities and fostering a sense of responsibility — in order to help teens transition away from home and learn what it's like to live on their own.

But there are a dizzying array of pre-college programs — sometimes called "summer camps" — to suit virtually every interest, ability and family budget, including:

- ACT and SAT Prep Programs
- Art and Music Programs
- Athletic Programs
- Business Programs
- Drama and Theater Programs
- Engineering Programs
- General Interest Programs
- Leadership Programs
- Literature and Writing Programs
- Math and Science Programs
- Special Education Programs
- Study Abroad Programs
- And more!

Regardless of the program's emphasis, however, most pre-college offerings give students a chance to experience the larger campus community, go on local field trips to areas of interest, or simply engage in extra-curricular activities that may or may not dovetail with various academic topics being studied.

Popular pre-college offerings run directly by well-known schools include programs at Brown University, Carnegie Mellon, Cornell University, Emory University, George Washington University, Johns Hopkins, New York University, and UC Berkeley, to name a few.

Some of the better-known, third-party packagers of pre-college programs are: Blueprint; Education Unlimited; Explo; Julian Krinsky Camps

& Programs; LEADership, Education and Development Program (former-ly LEAD Program), Summer Discovery, Summer Fuel and Summer Study, to name a few.

Prices can run the gamut, from free or extremely low cost to outra-geously expensive.

Other than price, there is sometimes one less obvious difference be-tween expensive pre-college offerings and their lower-cost or free brethren.

In a nutshell, programs originating directly from most colleges and universities will boast that their faculty leads class sessions and teaches stu-dents enrolled in pre-college programs. With third-party programs, that may or may not be the case. Ditto for some free or low-cost programs that sometimes hire outside instructors to do the work.

You will only know for sure by asking questions and carefully reviewing a program's printed materials and online information.

Personally, I wouldn't be overly concerned if my kid enrolled in a pre-college program, whether it was at a prestigious school like Stanford University (on a free, low-cost or full-pay program) or at Alabama's lesser-known *Samford* University (again, via a free, low cost or a full-pay program) — and the instructors were *not* from the campus in question. As long as the person teaching a pre-college program has the experience, proper academic credentials and background to stand in front of a class and successfully teach, it matters little to me whether he or she went to an "elite" college or currently teaches at one, but it's up to you to decide.

An Overview of Early College High Schools

Early College High Schools represent another pre-college option. But these aren't summer programs; these educate students year-round.

Early colleges are high schools (and even feeder middle schools), which give youth early exposure to the academic rigors of college. The goal is to promote college readiness, and cut the time and cost typically associated with getting a post-secondary degree.

At an "early college" high school, educators combine the curriculum typically learned in high school and the first couple years of college.

So when a student is in 9th and 10th grades, he or she will take college-prep type high school classes. Then, in 11th and 12th grades, students take college-level courses, earning both college and high school credit. Tuition at many early college high schools is free, which means the overall college tab is significantly reduced.

Jobs For the Future, a non-profit focused on college and career issues, launched the Early College High School Initiative in 2002, with funding from the Bill & Melinda Gates Foundation, the Carnegie Corporation of New York, the Dell Foundation, the Ford Foundation, the Lumina Foundation for Education, the W.K. Kellogg Foundation, the Walton Family Foundation, and other local foundations.

Thus far, the results of their efforts have been impressive, with Early College students outperforming their peers nationwide:

- 90% graduate high school vs. 78% of students nationally
- 94% earn free college credit while in high school
- 30% earn an Associate's degree or other post-secondary credential while in high school
- One year past high school, 21% of early college students had earned a (four-year) college degree, compare to 1% of other students

As of mid-2014, there were 280 early college high schools in 32 states, serving more than 80,000 students who are predominantly low-income youth, students of color, and first-generation college goers, according to Jobs For the Future (JFF).

JFF is now a partner in a major push to expand the number of early colleges in the U.S., helping to transform 56 high schools into early college schools that will serve 50,000 additional students, including many English language learners.

"Now that we've seen this work, and we have the hard data to prove that, our goal is to work with more school districts across the country to scale this up and bring it to places that don't know about early college programs," says Kathryn Young, National Director of Education Policy for JFF, which provides technical assistance to early college high schools, districts and states.

The growth of early college high schools is, in large part, a response to the escalating cost of a college education, Young says. But many students also enroll to increase their chances of academic and career success.

"A lot of students talk about the rigor, the small class atmosphere, as well as the
counseling and tutoring help they get with early college high schools. It's a much more personalized approach," Young notes. It also bolsters students' self-esteem.

"High school students will often say: 'I knew I was capable of doing this work, but I was never pushed and now I'm much more confident that I can do college level work,'" Young says.

Teen students exposed to college-level work are more likely to graduate high school, go to college, stay in college and earn better grades too, according to separate studies conducted by the American Institutes for Research, and the Community College Research Center at Teachers College, Columbia University.

The Skinny on Early Entrance Programs

Early Entrance Programs are higher education programs that allow younger students to enroll and attend school full time at a college or university campus. Students typically do not have to possess a high school diploma. However, the admission requirements, structure and the costs of these programs can vary greatly across institutions.

Among those early entrance programs that enroll high school students as full-fledged college freshmen, most charge the college or university's normal tuition. Many programs, however, do offer scholarships. And then there are some programs that are completely tuition free. That's the case, for example, at Bard Early College.

Additionally, some programs straddle high school and college curriculum, so the first two years is tuition-free; then, during their final two years, students pay the school's going tuition rates.

Besides Bard, which also boasts a network of free Bard High School Early Colleges, with affiliate schools in New York, New Jersey, Ohio, Louisiana, and Massachusetts, other well-known early entrance programs nationwide include:

- Transition School & Early Entrance Program at the University of Washington

- Early Entry Program at UCLA
- Boston University Academy at Boston University
- The Early College at Guilford at Guilford College
- Texas Academy of Mathematics and Science at the University of North Texas
- Early Honors Program at Alaska Pacific University
- Resident Honors Program at the University of Southern California
- National Academy of Arts, Sciences and Engineering at the University of Iowa

Currently, about 1.4 million students take classes annually for college credit while they are still in high school. That's up 67% over the past decade, according to The National Center for Education Statistics.

Regardless of whether they attend early college" high schools or Early Entrance Programs, the number of high school students enrolled in such programs may increase dramatically in future years if key financial issues are addressed.

Currently, while 70% of colleges and universities that offer dual and concurrent enrollment programs charge reduced tuition or no tuition to some or all students, 66% of postsecondary institutions report that some parents and students do contribute to tuition, according to data from the National Alliance of Concurrent Enrollment Partnerships (NACEP).

But there are efforts underway to allow high school students taking college classes to get federal college financial aid — something they can't do presently.

"Currently Pell grants, Stafford loans, and other Title IV federal student financial aid is not available for dual and concurrent enrollment because of a statutory prohibition on the use of such funds by students enrolled in high school," says Adam Lowe, executive director of the NACEP.

But the U.S. Department of Education has the authority to waive that statute and associated regulations for "**experimental sites**," Lowe notes.

And Lowe argues that banning high school students from getting college financial aid unfairly penalizes those students for starting college early.

That's why NACEP — which works to ensure that college courses taught by high school teachers are as academically rigorous as classes offered on the sponsoring college campus — has offered suggestions to the Education Department for possible experiments to allow students enrolled in dual and concurrent enrollment to access federal student financial assistance.

If NACEP's recommendations are approved, they could pave the way for tremendous economic support for high school students interested in taking college classes early.

College Secret:

High school students that take college classes may soon be eligible for federal financial aid — just like students already enrolled in U.S. colleges and universities.

The Role of College-Level Classes and College Credit Exams

There is a fourth and final category of pre-college work for high school students. These are the college-level classes and tests students can take while in high school, namely AP and IB classes, and CLEP exams. Some classes provide an end-of-year exam, which can result in college credit; others do not. But all these classes prepare students to be ready for the academic challenges of college life.

The AP or Advanced Placement Program

AP classes are college-level classes that teenagers take while in high school. At the end of the course, students take an exam, which is scored on a 1 to 5 point system.

A passing score for an AP exam is a 3. And if students get a "qualifying score," most colleges will offer college credit or advanced placement, allowing a student to skip an introductory course or fulfill a generation education requirement typically imposed on college freshmen.

Each school has its own criteria for a "qualifying score." But generally speaking, the vast majority of colleges and universities will accept a 3 as a "qualifying score." Most top schools in the country require a 4 or 5 on an AP exam in order to grant college credit. To know for sure, check out the website of the college(s) you're interested in, and review their policies on AP exams.

In the United States, AP exams cost $89 apiece to take. That may seem pricey, but it's a true bargain compared to the cost of taking a college class. (The fee for AP exams administered outside the U.S. is $119). If you score well enough an on AP exam, that test will save you hundreds (if not thousands) of dollars.

Unfortunately, not all high schools offer AP classes. If that's the case, you can still do independent study and take an AP exam at a nearby school that does offer the test.

If you look at a degree as a way to increase your earnings power, getting college credit as early as possible, through initiatives like the AP Program, "is really one of the best ways for high school students to reduce college costs," says Lucie Lapovsky, the former president of Mercy College and an expert on higher education finances.

AP Exam Subsidies Worth Thousands of Dollars

Just like with SAT and ACT tests, there are fee reductions and waivers available for AP exams. For those with economic need, you can get a $26 or $28 College Board fee reduction per AP Exam, depending on the state in which you attend school.

Additionally, many states heavily subsidize the cost of AP exams. It's a subsidy worth thousands and thousands of dollars, as I'll explain in detail momentarily.

But the main idea is that states supply federal and/or state funds to augment the College Board fee reduction, further lowering test costs. With these additional sources of aid, many income-eligible students will pay *nothing at all* to sit for an AP exam.

That's the case for low-income students in the following states: Arkansas, Connecticut, Indiana, Louisiana, Minnesota, North Carolina, South Carolina and Wisconsin. Their cost for the AP exam is: $0.

In fact, in Wisconsin, public school districts are required by law to pay for all AP Exam fees for students who qualify for free or reduced-price lunch. So income-eligible Wisconsin teens would get to take the AP exam completely free, even if the College Board didn't offer its own price break.

Elsewhere, other low-income students taking AP exams can pay as little as $5 (in California, Michigan and New Mexico) to $8 (in Alabama, Delaware, Illinois, and Vermont).

For eligible students in most other states, they can fork over just $10 to $31 to take an AP test, depending on their state of residence.

The most that a low-income student should pay to take an AP exam is $55 (for Nebraska and Washington D.C. residents) and $53 (for Florida, North Dakota, Utah and Wyoming students). But there are a few aberrations. For instance, in Oklahoma, depending on how officials handle it, student cost for AP exams may be $10, $56 or $64.

College Secret:

Low-income students in 15 states can take AP exams for free, or pay $5 or $8 for AP exams and get college credit for passing those tests.

The College Board's website provides a breakdown for the additional state funding available for AP testing, as well as what students' final out-of-pockets costs were in 2014. As with all things college-related, these costs may climb in subsequent years.

So you should always check the College Board's site for the latest information on AP exams. Alternatively, ask your school's AP coordinator or your high school counselor about any updates regarding waivers and federal or state aid for taking AP exams.

The $13,000 to $40,000 AP Savings Strategy

Just to recap and illustrate how powerful and cost-effective it can be to take AP exams — with or without fee waivers — let's say you're from Michigan, or any other state, but you'd like to attend the University of Michigan, Ann Arbor.

Now assume you take four AP exams during your high school years and you pass them all.

If you enroll as a student in the College of Literature, Science & the Arts, here is what your AP efforts could net you at the University of Michigan, in terms of both college credit, and actual dollars saved.

Getting a 3, 4 or 5 on the AP Chemistry exam will earn you 5 credit hours, and let you skip several intro Chemistry classes — which accelerates your progress towards graduation.

Earning a 3, 4 or 5 on the AP Biology exam will give you either 4 or 5 credit hours. These scores would also allow you to bypass taking one or two lower-level biology courses, permitting you to enroll in a more advanced biology class or just graduate sooner.

Scoring a 4 or 5 on an AP English exam will give you 3 credit hours.

And achieving a score of 4 or 5 on an AP History exam will give you 4 credit hours.

All told, you've just earned the equivalent of 16 to 17 credit hours — all while still in high school! Now let's translate those college credits into cold, hard dollars.

Like most campuses, at the University of Michigan, tuition and fees are based on a full-time credit hour load, and the university considers you full time if you take between 12 and 18 credit hours per term as an undergrad. (Students taking less than 12 credit hours pay for classes on a per credit hour basis, which was $690 for the first hour of part-time instruction in 2014-2015, and $510 for each additional part-time hour after that).

For the 2014-2015 Fall/Winter term, tuition at the University of Michigan was $13,142 for in-state students and $40,392 for out-of-state students.

So as you can see: by taking just four AP exams — and scoring well on them — you could have saved yourself the equivalent of more than $13,000 in tuition (or more than $40,000 in tuition if you're an out-of-towner).

And how much did it cost you? If you paid out-of-pocket for all four AP exams at full price, you shelled out exactly $356. That's a drop in the bucket compared to the many thousands in tuition savings you just netted.

Plus, if your family is low-income and you live in Michigan, you could take those four AP exams at the government-subsidized price of just 20 bucks — a measly $5 apiece!

Where else can you spend only $20 to save more than $13,000? It's a no-brainer anyway you slice it.

International Baccalaureate (IB) Diploma Programme

The International Baccalaureate (IB) Diploma Programme is a rigorous two-year program that grants students a special qualification when they graduate from high school. An IB diploma does not provide college credit, but it does prepare students for college-level work, and the IB program is known for its high academic standards.

Students whose schools offer IB coursework take these classes in the 11th and 12th grades. There are 800 high schools that offer the IB diploma in the U.S. Many of these schools are free, as they are public schools that are state-funded. Others schools with IB curriculum are private schools that charge tuition.

According to the website of the International Baccalaureate Organization: "IB curriculum is structured to address the intellectual, social, emotional and physical well-being of students, who must choose one subject from each of five groups (1 to 5), ensuring breadth of knowledge and understanding in their best language, additional language(s), the social sciences, the experimental sciences and mathematics. Students may choose either an arts subject from group 6, or a second subject from groups 1 to 5."

At the end of the program, students take a variety of assessments, including written exams, and then they are awarded a set number of points for their effort. IB students must earn at least 24 points for the IB diploma and a maximum of 45 can be earned.

The Importance of CLEP Exams

Developed by the College Board, the College-Level Examination Program, better known as CLEP, is a credit-by-examination program accepted by 2,900 colleges and universities worldwide.

There are a total of 33 CLEP exams, which test a student's mastery of introductory-level college material in a variety of categories: History and Social Sciences; Composition and Literature; Science and Math; Business; and World Languages.

CLEP exams cover material taught in courses that are typical for a freshman or sophomore in college. If you pass a 90-minute CLEP exam, you can earn anywhere from 3 to 12 college credits, depending on the subject matter.

Taking a CLEP exam costs $80, and 1,800 test centers administer the CLEP.

Just as with AP exams, CLEP exams are a phenomenally good deal — potentially saving you thousands of dollars — if you do well and then get credit for them at the college or university of your choice.

High school students (and even adults) prepare for CLEP exams through their general academic studies through significant independent study or through extracurricular work.

Although the vast majority of U.S. colleges and universities accept CLEP test credits, before you sit for a CLEP test, it's best to check directly with the college campuses of your choice to ask about their CLEP acceptance policies.

Unfortunately, there are no state programs or general waivers to reduce the cost of taking CLEP exams. But there are two federal assistance programs of note.

Under the first program, the federal government pays for CLEP exams for military personnel, some of their spouses, as well as civilian employees of the Army, Navy, Air Force, Marine Corps and U.S. Coast Guard (including active duty and reserve).

So if you happen to be in the military before entering college, investigate this cost-saving option and confirm your eligibility via the military's DANTES program. Military members can even get free CLEP exam guides and study materials to further reduce their test-related costs.

To take a CLEP exam free, you must test on a military base, at a college test center sponsored by a nearby military base, or at a test center identified as "Fully funded."

"Fully funded" test centers are those colleges and university test centers with agreements to waive their administrative fee for eligible service members and civilians whose exam fees are covered by DANTES (Defense Activity for Non-Traditional Education Support).

Secondly, if you are the son, daughter or spouse of a veteran who died, is disabled, went missing in action or was captured in the line of duty, you can qualify for a number of VA educational benefits including: free national testing (for the SAT, ACT, or CLEP); licensing and certification exams that are paid for; and college tuition that is fully covered by the federal government. So that is another way to have CLEP testing and other college costs covered.

You can determine your eligibility and apply for VA benefits at: http://www.ebenefits.va.gov.

Now that you know the range of academic pre-college options that exist, it's probably no wonder that scores of students are interested in these offerings.

But if you're considering possibilities for the summer, before you sign up for any pricey pre-college program, you should be clear about your objectives and what you hope to get out of the program.

You should also explore other summer activities that won't cost you a dime:

- Volunteering
- Doing an Internship
- Getting a Job
- Engaging in Distance Learning
- Conducting Independent Study

I'll discuss each of these free summer options in Chapter 6. But first: let's turn our attention to evaluating pre-college summer programs. You need to know what to look for, what programs will best serve your needs, and what to avoid.

CHAPTER 3

ᒣHE ᒣRUTH ABOUT PRE-COLLEGE SUMMER PROGRAMS

One way college-bound students try to get a leg up on the competition — and increase their chances of college admission — is by pursuing academic enrichment activities that go well beyond the typical high school curriculum.

Some students take college-level courses at nearby colleges and universities. Others pursue internships or partake in extracurricular research.

But one of the most popular strategies teens use to increase their college preparedness, and try to look good to admission officers, is enrolling in pre-college programs on various college campuses.

Well, I hate to be the bearer of bad news. But billions of dollars are being spent annually in a fruitless effort to show off the wrong way.

There are nearly 2,000 pre-college programs in America, not to mention plenty of study abroad opportunities and other international programs designed for high school students.

If you partake in these initiatives for the right reasons — and with eyes wide open — they can be enriching, even life-changing experiences. But are these programs likely to get you into the college of your dreams?

In a word: no.

"Attending a Harvard summer program will boost a high school student's chances of admission to Harvard. Right? Wrong!" said Bev Taylor, founder of The Ivy Coach, writing in a no-holds barred article on HuffingtonPost.com. "It's a common misconception, one that way too many parents and high school students buy into year after year. In actuality, it's not so different from little kids believing in the Tooth Fairy," she added.

College Secret:

Attending a pricey pre-college program does NOT give a student an edge when it comes to college admissions.

Even packagers of pre-college programs — the straight talking ones, that is — readily acknowledge what these programs can and can't be expected to do.

One of those straight talkers is Justin Laman, head of Blueprint Summer Programs, a leading provider of pre-college camps.

Blueprint offers teenagers the opportunity to experience a slice of life at a variety of college campuses, including George Washington University, Lehigh University, Stonehill College, UCLA, UC San Diego, and the University of Virginia.

Parents and students rave about Blueprint, but Laman candidly admits that these programs aren't for every teen.

In fact, he outlines the 5 *worst* motivations for attending a pre-college program:

1. Because you think attending the program will help you get into that college.

"Don't be fooled by fancy literature and promises that can't be kept! The way you get into college is through grades, classes, essays and test scores — not a pre-college program," Laman says. "There is no magic bullet. Pre-college programs are a tool for you to test-drive college, nothing more. If you go into yours with this mindset you'll get the most out of your pre-college experience. Trust us!"

2. Because my parents made me.

"Oh boy. Parents, don't do it. Don't sign them up just because you think it will be good for them. Have a family discussion about what your student wants. Sometimes a better option is a summer job, internship, travel or even just relaxing and being a kid."

Then again, Laman adds this word of caution to students: "Sometimes Mom does know best. (So) be open to the idea and at least consider a pre-college program with an open mind. Maybe they aren't for you, but check them out. They might be cooler than you think!"

3. Because you have nothing else better to do.

"This goes hand-in-hand with number 2 and we're 50/50 on it. If you have nothing better to do but *want* to go to a pre-college program, by all means," Laman suggests. "Just don't get sucked into the idea that you *have* to do one. What's your passion? What do you enjoy doing? Following your passions looks better on college apps than going through the motions."

4. Because you think it will look good on your college resume.

"First of all, we hate the idea that students actually have resumes these days but sometimes the rules change and you still have to play by them," Laman notes. "Unless your pre-college program is hyper-competitive and world renowned, most likely, no one is going to care that you attended. No offense!"

5. Because your boyfriend/girlfriend is going.

Give college a test-drive alone, Laman recommends. "Coming with someone from home is OK, but not someone who you want to spend every second of every day with. College and pre-college programs are a place and time to explore new things and discover new things about yourself too."

None of this is to suggest that students should never take a pre-college program or sign up for a worthwhile summer initiative. On the contrary, research shows that certain pre-college activities, such as taking college-level courses while still in high school, can have real academic and career benefits.

So the goal is to think carefully about these programs and their benefits, explore various alternatives, and then pursue your passions and interests in the most cost-efficient way.

To do this properly, you must first understand all of your options and know the differences between various types of pre-college initiatives.

Above all, it helps to understand the unvarnished truth about pre-college residential programs at many institutions.

A Skeptic's Point of View

Yes, the faculty, staff and administrators want to help educate young minds. And yes, many aspire to provide college-level exposure and a true college experience for teens.

But like many aspects of college, the typical pre-college program is primarily just a business, pure and simple. Call me a skeptic if you like, but it's true.

The over-arching goal of most pre-college programs is to fill empty dorm beds and make money from students who pay tuition. So pre-college summer programs are largely designed to be revenue generators — and really good ones, too.

College Secret:

Most colleges and universities run pre-college summer programs to generate revenue — not to spot academically talented students to later enroll in school.

The sooner you understand that reality, the sooner you can put certain things in proper perspective and take the right approach in picking a pre-college program.

What kinds of things need to be examined in the right context? For starters, the avalanche of pre-college mail you may have received, and/or the invitations from third-party marketers to attend various pre-college programs need to be taken not with a *grain* of salt, but a heaping dose of it.

Now I realize that you probably felt extra special when those big-name colleges reached out to you (or your child), right? And you may have delighted in finding your mailbox stuffed with fancy nominations to join "exclusive" societies; pre-college brochures promising to expose you to exciting international "opportunities;" or invitations to join very serious-sounding programs in Washington DC and elsewhere.

Well, I'm sure that you really are a great student and all, but make no mistake about what's going on here, why these colleges are contacting you, and how they go about doing it.

Andrew Ferguson, the author of *Crazy U: One Dad's Crash Course In Getting His Kid Into College,* explains the situation in plain English.

According to Ferguson, colleges buy lists of college bound students — mainly juniors but also now sophomores — from four sources: The College Board (which administers the SAT and which has a Student Descriptive Questionnaire in the PSAT); the ACT Inc. (the main competitor to the SAT); and two for-profit firms (which are in the list-building business and which get their information by mailing millions of questionnaires to high school teachers for distribution to their students). The cost is approximately 30 cents per name, Ferguson notes.

When students take standardized tests, they "give up their address, GPA, ethnicity, academic interests, and extracurricular activities. They estimate family income and disclose whether they expect to request financial aid," Ferguson says.

"Together, these four lists yield a mother lode of data about nearly every college-bound high school student in the United States," he adds.

This list-buying activity actually represents a tiny fraction of what colleges spend in order to put themselves in front of you and get your attention. There's also big dollars spent on catalogues, viewbooks, visits to high schools, and more.

Four-year colleges now spend an average of $2,311 on recruiting every student who enrolls, according to a report by the National Association for College Admission Counseling.

So here's the bottom line: colleges are spending a lot of money for a reason. They want to boost their rankings and they need to boost their yield: that is, the percentage of students enrolled versus the percentage of students they accept each year.

What's more, since most schools don't have enormous endowments, colleges are constantly in revenue-generation mode — yes, even *nonprofit* institutions.

Colleges and universities get money not just from donors, alumni, and students who enroll as freshmen, sophomores, juniors and seniors. They also get dollars from high school students and their families, who represent the next batch of willing consumers of education.

Peter Van Buskirk, who runs a popular blog called BestCollegeFit.com, put it best, in a blog post entitled "Too Good to be True?":

"If you are a high school student in grades 9-11, there is a very good chance you have begun to receive unsolicited messages from a range of organizations informing you of your nomination to be included in a special honor society or to attend summer leadership programs.

On the surface, such nominations are intriguing. In fact, what's not to like about them?! The very notion that you have been nominated to receive recognition for your achievements or to take advantage of extraordinary—not to mention seemingly exclusive—life experiences is almost too good to be true. It's good "ego food" and, who knows, maybe your participation will look good on your college applications.

Before you get too excited, let's take a closer look at what is going on with these "nominations."

They are being sent to you by organizations—businesses, to be sure— that seek to capitalize on the eager hopes and, in some cases, insecurities, of young people as they apply to college. The content that is being offered might be valid, but it is rarely as substantive or meaningful as the nomination would suggest.

A leadership week in Washington, D.C. could be a great experience (if you've never been to D.C. before), but it is certainly not exclusive. Doing volunteer work in Costa Rica sounds exotic and could make a difference in the lives of others—did I mention it sounds exotic?! Hmmm. And a listing with an honor society or "who's who" might make you feel good, but don't expect it to garner much attention in the admission process.

You see, the same "nomination" that you might have received was sent to tens of thousands of other students around the country.

Van Buskirk concludes with some matter-of-fact advice: "The program sponsors' objective is to sign you up," he says. So he offers several tips to consider as you evaluate the "nominations" that are bound to come your way:

1. **Beware of "who's who" distinctions and "honor" societies outside of your school for which you must pay to be recognized.** *You should never have to pay for a credential.* True honors are earned and will rightfully be bestowed upon you.

2. **Commit your time to others because it gives you joy to do so.** Admission officers are wary of volunteer experiences that can be bought. Remember, they are cynics—and the cynic will see vacation where you had hoped they would see volunteerism.

3. **If you are truly interested in doing community service over the summer—or any time, for that matter—look for opportunities to make a difference in your own community.** Participate in a Habitat for Humanity project. Serve meals to the homeless. Become a Big Brother/Big Sister. The hallmark of service is selflessness.

4. **Choose activities that will be truly enriching.** As you contemplate your options for discretionary involvement, do so as though applying to college is not in the picture. Choose those opportunities that will help you learn and grow. Admission officers look for authenticity in the person and character of the candidates they are considering. Let your choices be a window into the qualities you possess.

5. **Don't subscribe to special academic programs or camps for high school students on college or university campuses in order to help your chances of getting into those schools.** Keep in mind that, first and foremost, these programs are offered because the host institutions have empty beds to fill over the summer. Do the math. If a school can fill the beds with eager high school students over the course of two or three summer sessions, it will have succeeded in bringing thousands of students to its campus—a financial boon to the institution. Will any of those students be assured an advantage in the subsequent admission process? Maybe, but there are no guarantees. If you choose such a program, do so because it has

particular meaning to you. Following a prescribed course of activity simply to impress admission committees can otherwise be incredibly limiting.

Given the knowledge you now have, what's the best way to approach your pre-college summer options?

Let me give you a step-by-step overview explaining how you can successfully accomplish this task. Then I'll show you some real-life examples of my advice — and how following my recommendations can save you a boatload of cash.

How to Find Your Ideal Pre-College Option

Use the following seven steps and you'll find the right pre-college option, without breaking the bank:

Step #1: Write down what your goal is in attending a pre-college program.

Do you want a residential experience at a specific campus because that college or university is high on your list of target schools?

Are you interested in a pre-college program mainly as a way to test out a possible major or learn more about a subject of interest, such as science, fashion design, architecture or psychology?

Is a certain city or section of the country intriguing to you, or do you yearn to discover whether you'd prefer college life in a big city, small town or a rural environment? Or do you want to attend a pre-college program just to know what it's like to be in a true college setting, and really *any* campus will do?

Whatever your objective, write it down to be clear about your purpose and intent in finding the "right" pre-college program.

Step #2: Identify two to five colleges or universities of interest to you, then go to their websites and create a list of one or two pre-college programs they offer that you'd want to take.

Tips: Be sure to include at least one local college, but don't just limit your prospects to in-state campuses. (I'll explain why later.) For now, simply cast a wide net. If you have trouble coming up with a list of up to five colleges, don't worry about specific names. Just do an online search of the phrase "pre-college programs" and add some keywords to your search query to narrow your options. For example, if you're curious about an academic pre-college program that might be of interest to art history majors, search "pre-college programs" and "art history." Such a search would lead to you a variety of schools, including the Pratt Institute, Barnard College, and the Maine College of Art.

As part of your online research, find out the exact weekly price of the pre-college programs you've identified.

At this phase, don't let geography, finances or sticker-shock deter you or limit your search options.

If you find a program that truly interests you, put it on your list regardless of cost. Even if the campus is out of town, if the pre-college program is appealing to you and would help you meet your goal, add it as a potential summer program.

Note: this list should <u>only</u> include pre-college programs offered *directly* by colleges and universities themselves — not pre-college programs supplied by third-party entities, even if those programs are hosted on your target campus.

Step #3: Go find an alternative, *more affordable* pre-college option at the very same school(s) of interest to you.

Here's where you can add to your list and include pre-college programs run by outside companies or organizations, the firms I refer to as "third-party marketers" of pre-college experiences.

Realize that third-party marketers frequently have cheaper pre-college programs than colleges and universities offer, but that's not always the case. Your job is to locate a *less expensive* option than what the campus is offering directly.

How do you do this? In addition to third-party packagers of pre-college experiences, seek *different routes* into schools of interest: i.e. through minority programs' "pipeline" programs' enrichment opportunities targeting males or females; programs for talented youth; programs that help first-generation college students or teens from low-to-moderate income families; government or community funded pre-college programs, etc. (See examples of these, and a detailed explanation of how to find affordable pre-college programs following the seven steps in this section).

Step #4: Analyze the differences between direct college offerings and third-party programs that are hosted on a college campus.

Be objective in scrutinizing your options. Don't just fall hook, line and sinker for everything you read on a fancy website or in glossy brochures. And don't rule out a campus just because it's not in a certain category, such as being an Ivy League school or an elite, "brand-name" college or university that's well known.

Also, be honest in your evaluation of the differences among the pre-college programs you find.

Does it matter if you were to attend a program and most or all of the other participants were, say, from your own school, town/city or from the same state as you? What if everyone hailed from a different state or a different country than you? Would it bother you if other attendees were predominantly minority or low-income youth?

Would you be uncomfortable interacting with teens from different social, racial, religious, geographic or economic backgrounds? Or would you consider that an opportunity to learn and grow?

Would you care that one program has courses led by college faculty members while another has paid instructors who don't work for the campus?

And what about the structure of the programs? Are you most interested in academic or social activities? Does it have to be a residential offering, where you stay overnight in dorms? Or would you be fine with skipping the immersion experience, and attending a daytime only pre-college program where you commuted back home each day?

Finally, don't forget to evaluate the price differences among pre-college offerings. You can group pre-college programs into four different price categories:

   a. Free. These are "no tuition" programs, or sponsored programs where tuition and/or room and board is covered by benefactors, donors, corporations, the college itself, alumni or other parties.
   b. Low Cost: Programs that charge about $50 to $500 per week.

   c. Moderately Priced: Programs cost roughly $500 to $1,000 weekly.

   d. Expensive: Pre-college programs that charge $1,000 to $2,500+ per week.

Step #5: Consider the pros and cons of going with a "local" pre-college program that's actually out of your town or state.

Assume you're from Florida and you want to attend a music-focused pre-college program in Austin, Texas — a city that bills itself as "The Live Music Capital of the World." The pre-college program you like is called "The Texas Musical Summer Institute" and it appears to only target teens from greater Austin area or the entire Lone Star State (Texas).

Before you dismiss such a program based on the assumptions that it's out of your district or state and it accepts only "local" students, call and ask whether they'd consider taking an out-of-state student. Sometimes slots don't fill up, or the program may welcome the chance to expose its local students to youth from other areas.

Step #6: Inquire about scholarships and tuition discounts at all programs.

Always, always ask about fee reductions, such as full or partial scholarships offered by a pre-college program. You'd be surprised at how many programs simply don't widely advertise the availability of such funds, but there is money to help students nonetheless. Financial support usually comes from the organization itself, non-profits and corporations, as well as patrons who may be alumni or generous benefactors who want to promote college access.

When there is absolutely no money available, a pre-college program will usually say so on its website — typically under the tuition and fees section, or in the FAQ area. If scholarship information isn't found on the site, you stand a good possibility that the program may indeed offer discounts based on:

- Financial need
- Merit and accomplishment
- Personal essays
- Geographic preferences
- Racial, ethnic or socio-economic diversity

- Early enrollment
- Multiple siblings
- Return students
- ... and more

So remember to <u>always ask</u> directly about price breaks and tuition discounts, especially if you can't find such info online. The worst that can happen is that they say there are no scholarships or discounts available.

Tip: It's best to start looking for pre-college summer programs during the late fall and early winter seasons. That way you can narrow your list, investigate scholarships if necessary, and be prepared to fill out applications and scholarship forms right around January.

Competitive summer pre-college programs that get a lot of applications (including those for talented youth, and many free offerings) have early deadlines — starting in December or January and culminating in March or April. Many others' programs, though, have late spring deadlines, rolling deadlines, or some may have deadlines right up until the pre-college program starts or becomes full.

Whatever the case, it's always much safer and wiser to apply *as early as possible*, especially if you're seeking funding. Many pre-college programs provide their scholarships and grants on a "first come, first served" basis, handing out scholarship funds until that money is exhausted.

Step #7: Seek financial aid through college access groups, foundations and educational organizations.

If necessary, take time to seek financial aid through organizations and foundations that offer economic assistance to students who want to enroll in pre-college programs. Some of these resources include:

Achievement First
Bright Futures
Graduation Generation
Jack Kent Cook Foundation
Joyce Ivy Foundation
Minds Matter

QuestBridge
Schuler Scholar Program
Summer Search

Most of these groups require you to submit a scholarship application between January and March in order to receive aid for the summer. So if your goal is to attend a pricey pre-college program, but you can't afford it, I would urge you again to get to work on your funding request early.

If you follow the seven steps I've just outlined, you can definitely find an affordable pre-college program — even many *free* ones — that meet your needs.

Don't believe me? Just keep reading for more truly eye opening and money-saving information.

CHAPTER 4

$\mathcal{N}$O-COST AND LOW-COST PRE-COLLEGE PROGRAMS

Have you set your sights exclusively on the popular paid pre-college programs offered directly by well-known colleges and universities across the country? If so, you can expect to shell out big bucks for these pre-college experiences, as I'll now illustrate.

Let's say you have an interest in a business-oriented program. Here's what a half-dozen top schools recently charged for their pre-college summer programs:

Emory University had a 6-week program, the Emory Institute for Data Science, which paired students with faculty in Economics, and granted 4 college credits.
Cost: $9,689 or $1,567 per week.

Harvard offered a 7-week program, via its Secondary School Program, with courses like Principles of Economics and International Relations, which granted 8 credits.
Cost: $11,000 or $1,571 per week.

New York University had a 6-week program, Summer @ Stern, awarding students 8 credits for taking two classes like Business Essentials or Business and Investing.
Cost: $11,651 or $1,942 per week.

Northwestern had a 6-week College Prep Program that included an Intro to Macroeconomics class and a Marketing Management course, granting students the equivalent of 6 college credits.
Cost: $10,000 or $1,667 per week.

University of Southern California offered high school students a 4-week course, Exploring Entrepreneurship, which awarded 3 college credits.
Cost: $7,416 or $1,854 per week.

University of Pennsylvania had a 6-week program that provided students with the equivalent of 6 credits for taking two courses, including Intro to Microeconomics.
Cost: $13,299 or $2,217 per week.

Are you seeing a pricing trend here? At many elite U.S. schools, it's common to spend about $1,500 to $2,000 *weekly* for the privilege of attending residential pre-college programs.

Why are some parents willing to spend small fortunes on these pre-college experiences?

Many are no doubt wealthy parents who feel like they're just paying for the very best education that money can buy. Others may have more shallow motivations. They just want bragging rights, and to be able to say: "My kid is spending the summer at _____ (fill in the blank with a brand-name college or university)."

But for most families, I suspect that they spend all this money due to three factors.

For starters, many parents simply don't know any better. They don't realize that plenty of excellent colleges and universities (including the ones I just listed), actually have *free* summer options and lower-cost pre-college programs, too.

Additionally, too many parents mistakenly think that enrolling their kid in a pre-college program at ultra-selective colleges like Harvard will somehow make that child a shoo-in — or at least give him or her a competitive edge — as a college applicant.

But even Harvard officials, who are no doubt aware of this misconception, try to dispel this myth. On its pre-college website, Harvard notes:

"There is no relation between admission to the Harvard Summer School Secondary School Program and admission to the freshman class at Harvard College."

The $2,000 Test Drive

There is a third, and somewhat practical reason, however, that some parents bite the bullet financially and pay for their child to take a pricey pre-college program.

Justin Laman, of Blueprint, sums it up this way: "Some parents would rather make a $2,000 investment now to make sure they don't make a $200,000 mistake down the road."

Laman's point is that it's far cheaper to let a teen "test drive" a college now, rather than find out after several years later that the student is dropping out or wants to change schools because he or she didn't like the college or it wasn't the right fit.

Laman's point is well taken. And I don't blame well-heeled families for making that investment to help their kids really get to know a campus before applying. Nevertheless, for parents who *can't* afford the $2,000 test drive, there is — thankfully — a much better way.

It only requires two things: for you to open your mind to various creative possibilities, and to do your homework.

Free and Low-Cost Summer Options — Even at Ivy League Schools

I've just showed you how expensive it can be to attend some pre-college programs run by top schools.

Now what if I told you that you could attend a pre-college program at some of these same schools, or other prestigious schools, for a fraction of the price — or even no money at all?

It's true. Let's take another look at various pre-college options, this time highlighting a half-dozen *free* pre-college business programs.

Bryant University runs a pre-college summer business program, known as the PricewaterhouseCoopers Accounting Careers Leadership Institute.

Since PWC sponsors the Institute, students pay nothing to participate. Applicants must be African-American or Latino students who are high school juniors (i.e. rising seniors).
Cost: $0.

Indiana University, Bloomington hosts two different free one-week programs called the Young Women's Institute and MEET Kelley, through the Kelley School of Business. The first program targets females; the latter program is directed toward under-represented minorities, including African-American, Latino, Native American and Native Hawaiian/Pacific Islander students.
Cost: $0.

North Carolina A&T State University offers two free, residential programs to high school students, and one free commuter program, called the Agribusiness Institute. The programs are 4 weeks, 1 week and 8 days, respectively, and are offered via the School of Agriculture and Environmental Sciences. Amazingly, some of these programs even offer stipends, essentially paying teenagers for being good students and learning at the campus.
Cost: $0.

Seattle University provides a weeklong but robust Summer Business Institute via its Albers School of Business and Economics. The program is designed for under-represented students, including African-Americans, Latinos and Native Americans.
Cost: $50.

The Foundation for Teaching Economics sponsors Economics for Leaders, a free, one-week summer program that takes place on a variety of campuses and is geared toward rising seniors with leadership potential.
Cost: $0*

Note: While housing, meals and tuition for the program are all free, participants must pay a "program fee" that varies, depending on the campus chosen. In 2014, campus program fees ranged from $600 (at University of

Dallas) to $1,400 (at Yale University). Other schools included Vanderbilt ($750), William and Mary ($850), UC Berkeley ($1,000), and Duke University ($1,200), to name a few.

University of Texas at Austin offers not just one, but *two*, free weeklong programs sponsored by Ernst & Young through the McCombs School of Business.

The first program, called McCombs Future Executive Academy (MFEA), lets attendees explore various facets of a business degree and a career in business. The second program, called DYNAMC (Discover Yourself in Accounting Majors and Careers), exposes teens to a broad variety of accounting careers, from working at one of the Big Four global accounting firms to working for the FBI.

All students residing in the U.S. may apply. But the university especially encourages outstanding African-American, Hispanic and Native American students, as well as those who have overcome any social or economic hardship, to apply.
Cost: $0.

University of Washington offers ACAP, or the Accounting Career Awareness Program, a one-week free residency program at the university's Foster School of Business. The program targets minority applicants.
Cost: $0.

Wabash College provides a free, weeklong program dubbed OLAB, Opportunities to Learn About Business, for rising 12th graders considering a business major. Though Wabash is an all-male liberal arts college, the OLAB program is coed and all students are welcome to apply, regardless of race, gender or intended career choice.
Cost: $0.

I could go on, but you probably get the point: you don't always have to fork over big dollars just to attend a really good pre-college program.

What's the Difference Between Costly Pre-College Programs and Free Ones?

You may have noticed three key differences between the pricey pre-college programs I first mentioned and the latter, free ones.

First, the high-cost programs usually award college credit, whereas the cheaper programs typically don't. That wouldn't be a deal-breaker in my book — not by any stretch of the imagination — especially since you learned earlier in this chapter that the most cost-effective ways to get college credit are through AP testing and CLEP exams. So you don't need a pricey pre-college program just for college credits.

Besides, you can find *free* pre-college programs that offer college credit as well.

Consider **Caldwell College** in New Jersey. It runs Summer College at Caldwell, a free three-week pre-college program for high school juniors to study science, medicine and math. Applicants must be first-generation college students. They earn 3 college credits at no cost because funding for the program comes from the U.S. Department of Education College Access Challenge Grant through the New Jersey Commission on Higher Education.

In New York, all high school students attending public schools can take college-level classes free of charge through College Now, the country's largest dual enrollment and college readiness program. College Now is a growing collaboration between more than 350 New York schools with over 20,000 students and CUNY, the City University of New York. Under most circumstances, when students take courses via College Now, those credits transfer directly within the CUNY system. Similarly, many colleges and universities outside CUNY also accept credits from CUNY campuses.

A second key difference is that the free and/or lower-cost pre-college programs are largely designed to promote racial, ethnic, gender and socioeconomic diversity.

And finally, the free, sponsored programs you'll find are typically much shorter in duration, with most spanning one-week or so, instead of 6 weeks.

But does that mean that *all* free pre-college options fall into the category of shorter programs? Absolutely not.

And for those of you thinking: "Great, I'm not a minority, so there are no free options for me," that's not the case at all.

While it's true that the majority of free or subsidized programs are designed to help minorities, economically disadvantaged students or underrepresented youth, it's also the case that pre-college program sponsors recognize the need for diverse students of all backgrounds. They also want to foster college access at many levels.

You may not be a low-income student, and you may not be part of an ethnic or racial minority, but you may possess other unique qualities or special talents and interests that would make you an attractive candidate for pre-college programs.

Additionally, colleges and sponsors with an interest in promoting higher education are keen to help high-ability students who have a passion for learning, but need an expanded platform or more intensive options for learning. As a result, students of all backgrounds can earn acceptance into free pre-college programs. You just have to know where to look, and how to package yourself in the proper way.

Remember: colleges are looking to build a mosaic of students from all walks of life; that's one way they create more vibrant communities and the best possible exchange of ideas and knowledge.

"There's a diversity of perspective and thought that I think schools are looking to create for each of their campuses," says Aramis Gutierrez, who runs a pre-college program at Rutgers University.

Karen Richardson, the Associate Director of Admissions at Tufts University, who is also the school's Director of Diversity Recruitment, agrees.

"When you say the word 'diversity,' most students and parents seem to automatically think about just racial and ethnic diversity," Richardson says. "But we talk about diversity in a very broad sense."

According to Richardson, Tuft's philosophy of building a diverse, inclusive campus means also considering diversity of thought, and a host of other factors, such as socioeconomic status, sexual orientation, religious background, geographic residency and more. The campus even tries to ensure that it has a mix of students that represent diverse types of schools, such as public, private, charter, religious and home-schooled students.

"All of those things are important to make a dynamic campus atmosphere," Richardson says.

College Secret:

Any student can find a free or low-cost pre-college program just by doing the necessary research and approaching the selection process the right way.

To further demonstrate my point, let's stop looking at business-focused programs and take a look at programs of interest to students with a variety of academic or professional interests. As you can see, you can find a variety of free and low-to-moderate cost pre-college programs in every state and across every type of campus.

Here are some notable ones to consider, starting with several Ivy League schools:

Harvard offers a free summer 7-week program called the Crimson Summer Academy to local students who attend high schools in Boston or Cambridge.

Princeton University runs a Summer Journalism Program, a no-cost, 10-day program for low-income students that are rising seniors. There's also the tuition-free, multi-year Princeton University Program in Teacher Preparation, called the Princeton University Preparatory Program, or PUPP. It's a rigorous academic program that aids high-achieving, low-income high school students from local districts.

Brown University, another Ivy League school, offers Dean's Scholarships to cover pre-college program costs.

And there are two nifty things about Brown's pre-college programs:

1. They are geared toward students in grades 6 through 12. So even younger students can participate. Parents of middle school kids: start planning early!
2. Brown's pre-college programs also take place in three ways: on campus, online, and abroad, and there are scholarships available for each.

And what about Penn? Remember the hefty price tag for its pre-college program? Well, you could have another very similar pre-college experience at Penn, for far, far less.

Just look into the LEADership, Education and Development Program.

LEAD's Summer Business Institute is for rising seniors who want to attend prestigious campuses like the University of Chicago and University of Pennsylvania. The cost for 4 weeks at Penn via LEAD: it's $2,800, or $700 per week.

Recall that, by comparison, if you went to Penn's website and enrolled in their pre-college program for high school students, the 4-week residential program with two courses for credit would cost you $13,299 (or $10,299 if you only wanted to take one class for credit).

One other word of advice to parents with *younger* children who may have their hearts set on sending their kids to Ivy League colleges or other top schools when they reach college age — It would behoove you to encourage your children to not only be good students during the school year, but to not slack off during the summer.

They certainly never *need* to go to pre-college programs directed towards middle school students, but it's a good idea to keep them active and engaged during the summer — and not in front of the TV all day.

Fortunately (or unfortunately, depending on your perspective), the "pre-college" environment is gradually and continually pushing downward into the lower grades.

The one good thing about this expansion of the definition of what "pre-college" means is that there are more no-cost, academic summer programs than ever before for middle-school students, especially in math and science.

For instance, The ExxonMobil Bernard Harris Summer Science Camp is a free, two-week summer residential program at the New Jersey Institute of Technology that offers activities, experiments, projects, and field experiences for students entering 6th, 7th, or 8th grade in the fall. The camp promotes science, technology, engineering and mathematics (STEM) education and supports historically underserved and underrepresented students with limited opportunities.

For older teens in high school, another terrific — and free — summer science program is The Summer Science Institute (SSI) held at the

University of Wisconsin-Madison's Institute for Biology Education. This popular six-week residential experience helps students develop an understanding of biological and physical research. The program also boosts participants' writing and math skills. SSI is open to all students, but minority applicants, first generation students and youth from low-income families are especially encouraged to apply.

Here are a handful of other free and low-cost pre-college programs for minorities, just to give you an inkling of what's available.

Free and Low-Cost Summer Programs for Minorities

Carleton College runs a highly competitive weeklong residential program called the Carleton Liberal Arts Experience in Northfield, MN. The program, only available to the country's top African-American high school students, is totally free. Carleton even pays a student's travel costs to and from the college.

Carnegie Mellon University offers a free and highly regarded 6-week Summer Academy for Minority Students. While this residential science and math program is well known for being intensive, and very competitive to get in, Carnegie Mellon also has a number of other lesser-known but still excellent pre-college programs through its Summer Programs for Diversity. Those other free pre-college options include offerings in Advanced Placement/Early Admission (for college credit); Architecture; Art & Design; Drama; Music; and even a National High School Game Academy exploring the skills needed to be successful in the video gaming industry.

Massachusetts Institute of Technology provides exceptional students with six weeks of tuition-free study at the Minority Introduction to Engineering, Entrepreneurship, and Science program, better known as MITES. MIT also has a much-lauded Research Science Institute, open to students of any background, which likewise has a 6-week no-cost residential program next generation of science rock stars. A final one-week residential available as well for other talented minority students. Called the ng Experience at MIT, it too is offered at no charge.

QuestBridge Summer Program is a highly sought after five or six-week pre-college program with all expenses paid at dozens of top colleges and universities in the country. Students can attend a variety of highly ranked institutions, ranging from Amherst College, University of Chicago, Stanford University and Yale University to Bowdoin College, Columbia University, Vassar College and Wesleyan University. Quest Scholars must be low-income but high-performing students. Even better, successful Quest Scholars are matched with elite institutions that agree to provide full financial aid or a "free ride" to support four years of higher education.

Telluride Association Summer Programs include two programs, known as TASS and TASP, that rank among the country's premier pre-college summer experiences. For six weeks, students study on top-notch campuses, engaging in seminars that explore different themes in the humanities and social sciences. These free summer programs often focus on issues of race and have recently taken place on three campuses: Cornell University, Indiana University and University of Michigan, Ann Arbor. No grades or college credits are given. The programs are designed to simply foster a love of learning and deep scholarly and social inquiry. Telluride targets students from underprivileged and historically under-represented groups. But TASS and TASP applicants need not be minority students; they only need to demonstrate an interest in African-American studies.

Sewanee: The University of the South recently offered a free two-week program in Asian Studies called FACES, or Freeman Asian Cultural Experiences at Sewanee. Another no-cost program, the Bridge Program in Math and Science at Sewanee, is a three-week residential experience for rising high school seniors of diverse backgrounds. Sewanee is a selective liberal arts college located in rural Tennessee.

Virginia Military Institute offers the College Orientation Workshop (COW), a free, four-week program targeting minority male youth, especially African-Americans, who are rising juniors or seniors in high school.

You may or may not qualify or be interested in any of the programs mentioned in this chapter. But I've already shared a seven-step process for finding quality pre-college programs. So you can use your own research to track down our best options. You should also know of several tricks that can help you along the way. So keep on reading to discover additional ways to cut pre-college program expenses during your high school years.

CHAPTER 5

STRATEGIES TO SLASH PRE-COLLEGE PROGRAM EXPENSES

There are plenty of other strategies that students of all backgrounds (and ages) can use to lower their pre-college program costs.

For example, if you just want to learn a subject and don't necessarily require the overnight immersion experience, why not consider a daytime only pre-college option? These are often referred to as "commuter" or "non-residential" programs.

There are plenty of excellent commuter programs, even at top schools, that aren't in the typical $1,500 to $2,000 a week range. In fact, these classes-only alternatives are priced at a fraction of the cost of their residential program counterparts.

At the University of Virginia, a non-residential pre-college course of study involving two summer classes for 6 credits cost $2,358 over a six-week period. That works out to about $667 per week. Not cheap, but certainly not overly expensive, either.

It's also a lot less than what UVA charged for a new, 4-week residential program it launched in 2014, called UVA Advance, which also included two classes for six credits, along with room and board, workshops and field trips. Inaugural program fees for UVA Advance were $4,888, or $1,222 weekly for Virginia residents — not to mention twice the cost ($9,999 or $2,500 a week) for non-Virginians.

Commuter Programs Save Big Bucks

Elsewhere in Virginia, **The College of William and Mary** also offered a residential pre-college option, a 3-week program in Early American History that granted 4 credits and likewise included field trips to historic sites. The cost: $3,950 or $1,317 weekly for residents — and $4,150 or $1,383 weekly — for non-residents.

But a high school teen who received permission to take one summer class at William and Mary (without the residential portion), and received the same 4 credits, would have paid just $1,380 for a 5-week American History course, or $276 a week.

Then there's the University of North Carolina at Chapel Hill, which offered 6-week summer courses (5.5 weeks to be exact) to in-state commuters for just $690 apiece. Students taking one class earned 3 units. The cost worked out to just $115 per week. Adding on-campus housing into the mix, however, tacked on another $846. So opting to commute was a big money-saver.

College Secret:

Most students can save 50% to 80% off a pre-college program by taking the commuter option, instead of choosing the residential program experience.

Consider Lesser-Known Colleges To Cut Pre-College Costs

Another tactic when you simply want to learn about a subject or get exposure to a topic, is to target schools *away* from large cities, and consider campuses that aren't necessarily "brand name" institutions. Many colleges and universities outside of major metro areas — along with suburban, rural or just lesser-known campuses — often run outstanding pre-collegiate programs.

One terrific pre-college program is the Summer Honors Program at Indiana University of Pennsylvania. Hosted by IUP's Cook Honors College, the program gives students a chance to study whatever they're interested in — from archaeology, biochemistry, and from law to film and television, journalism or East Asian culture. And thanks to a generous alumni base, the college is able to offer $1,000 scholarships to all attendees, bringing down the cost of this 2-week residential program to just $300 — or $150 a week.

Elon Academy, at Elon University in North Carolina, is another stellar pre-college program and it's free of charge. Originally launched and funded by Elon itself, the Academy is now supported by the generosity of businesses, foundations and individuals. Elon Academy serves promising local high school students who have financial need or no family history of college. Recent scholars at Elon Academy have spent their summers studying criminal justice, creating writing, philosophy, engineering, ancient philosophy and more. The program's multi-year summer residential experiences are rounded out with year-round Saturday programs for students and their families. In recent years, three Elon Academy participants have won the prestigious and coveted Gates Millennium Scholarship, covering all college expenses.

Get Pre-College Funding Help From Uncle Sam

Another strategy for finding free and low-cost pre-colleges: go with a government or quasi-government sponsored program, one that is funded by state or federal resources. Examples include:

CDC Disease Detective Camp

This is a free, weeklong commuter program sponsored by the David J. Sencer CDC Museum in association with the Smithsonian Institution. The focus of the CDC Disease Detective Camp is public health and the science of epidemiology. (For middle school students, there is also a separate Junior CDC Disease Detective Camp that runs for three days and is likewise free of charge.) The camps are held at CDC headquarters in Atlanta and are open to all U.S. high school juniors and seniors at least 16 years old.

GEAR UP

GEAR UP is a federally funded program that prepares students for college success. GEAR UP stands for Gaining Early Awareness and Readiness for Undergraduate Programs.

These free offerings can be found at scores of good campuses across America, such as **Texas A&M University**, which provides GEAR UP "College Ready Camps" for local youth who aspire to achieve a higher education.

The National Council for Community and Education Partnerships maintains a Web-based GEAR UP Program Locator.

College Secret:

High school students can attend pre-college summer programs 100% free, courtesy of the U.S. government.

Governor's Schools

Governor's Schools are special summer programs for gifted students that are fully or partially funded by state legislatures and/or governor's offices. As a result, most are free; but some do have modest tuition charges.

In order to attend a governor's school you must be a resident of a state that offers this program. There are currently about two-dozen U.S. states with Governor's Schools, including Alabama, California, Florida, Georgia, New Jersey, New York, North Carolina, Pennsylvania, and Virginia.

These programs are typically residential in nature; but some are commuter programs. Also, while governor's schools vary by state, they are usually hosted on college or university campuses, giving high-achieving teens the chance to develop intellectually and socially.

The National Conference of Governor's Schools is the national organization of summer residential governor's school programs. At their website you can find links to Governor's School Programs by state.

NSLI-Y

The National Security Language Initiative for Youth, or NSLI-Y, is a free study abroad program for high school students sponsored by the U.S. State Department. The goal is to teach students one of seven lesser-known languages: Chinese (Mandarin), Hindi, Arabic, Russian, Korean, Turkish, and Persian (Tajik).

The NSLI-Y pre-college option is a not only residential program; it's also an intensive language immersion experience in a variety of locations around the world. And best of all: because it's backed by a federal agency, it's free for students accepted into this highly selective program.

TriO Programs

TriO programs are federally backed educational opportunity outreach programs designed to assist students from disadvantaged backgrounds. There are eight TriO programs in the United States, including three directly targeting elementary, middle-school and high-school aged youth:

- Educational Talent Search
- Upward Bound
- Upward Bound Math-Science

These programs vary in length and structure, but many offer no-cost, multi-week residential programs for pre-college students at colleges and universities across the country. They also include additional academic instruction, tutoring and ongoing educational support services throughout the school year.

For example, the Upward Bound Program at the **University of Maryland** has two parts: a six-week residential summer session (with classes in math, science, composition, foreign language and more), as well as year-round academic sessions to complement summer activities.

In general, to qualify for an Upward Bound or Talent Search program, a student must meet the federal guideline for "low income" or must be a "first-generation student" who is college bound. The definition of "first generation student" means the parent(s) living in a student's household does/do not have a Bachelor's degree.

The National College Access Network has an online program directory that lists college access programs (including TriO programs) by state.

More Pre-College Search Tips

If you ever face difficulty finding pre-college programs, there are several good online resources to help you track down the right one. These online sites include:

- http://www.enrichmentalley.com
- http://www.studenteducationprograms.com
- http://www.Usummer.com

And if the program you want to attend doesn't offer full scholarships or deep discounts, don't neglect to seek other funding sources. Check with your local PTA, religious organizations and faith-based groups, as well as civic associations, such as Alumni Associations, Kiwanis, Lions, Rotary, and more.

Local, regional and national organizations devoted to promoting college access can also be a wealth of information — and a fantastic source for funding as well. These groups often have dollars to make your pre-college program dreams a reality, or if they don't offer scholarship dollars directly, they can point you in the right direction for funding.

For example, at the regional level, Our Next Generation offers scholarships to students in the greater Milwaukee area to help support their attendance in pre-college programs:

Street Squash provides scholarships for summer camps and pre-college programs to youth in Harlem and Newark.

And the Assistance League of Seattle has an "Enrichment Scholarship Program" that provides scholarships for summer programs available to Seattle Public School children, grades 6 to 11. Students can pursue activities and academics in numerous fields such as music, art, science, mathematics, language, drama, technology, leadership, and outdoor experiences.

So be sure to do an online search of phrases like: "pre-college scholarship application" or "pre-college tuition scholarship" along with the name of the city or state in which you live.

Time Invested = Dollars Saved

Is all this too much work to do? No, not in the slightest — especially for the payoff your efforts will generate.

I'm asking you to make an investment in yourself, an investment of time that will save you and your family thousands and thousands of dollars. Isn't a few hours, or even a few days' worth of research and information gathering worth that?

How I Saved More than $4,000 on My Kids' Pre-College Programs

For example, when my oldest daughter expressed an interest in going to a pre-college program at my alma mater, the University of Southern California, I gladly obliged. Her goals were three-fold: to check out USC and see if she liked the campus, to determine if she'd be OK living so far away from home, and also to boost her public speaking skills.

I could have signed her up for the shortest program offered directly from USC. That was a two-week residential program that cost about $3,500.

But I knew there had to be more affordable options.

Sure enough, we found a local program, called the California Youth Think Tank (CYTT). It offered a one-week leadership program at USC designed to help students prepare for college and career success, and get to know USC's campus. Just like USC's program, students of CYTT enjoyed stimulating classes and activities, got official USC student ID cards and stayed for a week in USC dormitories.

On the surface, CYTT appeared to be only for students of the Golden State. But when I called the Program Director, William Young, who has run CYTT for more than two decades, he told me he would welcome an application from a New Jersey student.

My daughter applied, got in, and had a wonderful experience, which included making public presentations and participating in a student debate team during the program. The price? Less than $500, a small fraction of the cost our family would have paid by going directly through USC. Money saved: $3,000.

Another time, when researching summer programs for my son, who is an outdoor enthusiast and loves the wilderness, I discovered a real low-cost gem: 4H Youth Development Programs.

In my region, the Lindley G. Cook 4-H Youth Center for Outdoor Education, is a low-to-moderate cost outdoor education camp operated by Rutgers Cooperative Extension of Rutgers University. Participants are not required to be 4H members.

During the most recent summer, a weeklong camp program was just $550, with $50 discounts for many attendees, including early bird registrants, 4H members, military members, and Rutgers employees, as well as those with siblings enrolled.

But I actually found an even lower-cost option for my outdoor loving son: a weeklong program run by a non-profit called The Children of the Earth Foundation. I barely believed my eyes when I saw online that they were offering a special price of just $100 for a 6-day program for teens interested in a "survival camp." (The normal price was originally $695 for the week).

At Children of the Earth, youth, teens and families learn the ancient art and science of tracking, awareness, and wilderness living skills. Not only did my 14-year-old jump at the chance to attend, but my husband and I gladly drove our son the nearly two hours it took to get from our home in New Jersey to the multi-acre campsite in Holmes, New York.

After making his own survival shelter from materials in the forest and staying in it overnight, finding and purifying water in the woods, creating fire from nature and learning how to identify more than a half dozen wild, edible plants, my teenager grew up so much and came home completely enchanted by the entire experience. "It was amazing," my son told me.

Then he pleaded with us to let him attend the camp for *another* week. His father and I agreed. So I dropped my son off at camp again, where he learned even more, including how to track animals and humans based on prints left on the ground. Again, all of this cost a mere $100 a week.

Mind you, I was initially prepared to spend $550 a week at 4H or to at least *consider* the $695 weekly cost at Children of the Earth. Then the $100 a week offer made it a no-brainer. Total cash saved: about $1,200.

So make no mistake about it: both free and low cost pre-college programs of all kinds do exist. And some of them are truly life changing.

Do the Program Shuffle

Here's yet another creative way to find a cost-effective pre-college program when you hope to be at a specific college or university but are undecided about a major or a career choice. I call this method "the Program Shuffle."

In a nutshell, it involves taking a look at *all* the various pre-college offerings a campus provides — not just the ones the college or university showcases on the home page of its pre-college program website. Sometimes, the price difference among programs is shocking.

Notre Dame's pre-college programs are a perfect example.

Here's what students and their families were asked to pay for various pre-college programs, all taking place at Notre Dame in the summer of 2014.

If you went online to Notre Dame's Office of Pre-College Programs, you would have found two wonderful programs prominently featured on the site's home page:

The Notre Dame Leadership Seminars were 11-day residential programs sponsored by the college and offered free of charge to talented, rising high school seniors. Notre Dame even paid the students' transportation costs to and from the campus, and granted students one college credit.

By comparison, Notre Dame's Summer Scholars Program was a two-week residential offering that provided one college credit, and cost $3,100.

Both programs offered exceptional learning opportunities and were competitive. But one was sponsored free, while the other required tuition and fees.

What about other pre-college offerings from this distinguished school? Actually, there were plenty of other options, varying in cost and focus.

Notre Dame's PAN (Physics of Atomic Nuclei) Program is a free week-long residential summer camp for high school students, which takes place at the Nuclear Science Laboratory (NSL) at Notre Dame. The program is run by the Joint Institute for Nuclear Astrophysics (JINA) and NSL.

Notre Dame's Vision Program for students who want to learn about God's role in their lives is a five-day residential program that cost $450 or $475, depending on how early you submitted your application.

Notre Dame's Intro to Engineering Program is a two-week residential program for rising seniors that cost $1,850.

Notre Dame's Career Discovery for High School Students is a 13-day residential study initiative focused on architecture that cost $1,900.

And Notre Dame's International Leadership, Enrichment and Development Program is a 15-day program that cost $3,500.

So if you're not totally wed to pursuing one particular course of study, but you are very interested in a specific campus, do you see how doing the "program shuffle" — that is, being open to various programs and weighing all your options — could be a big money saver?

College Secret:

Students can sometimes cut their pre-college program expenses in half, just by being flexible about which summer option they choose at a given college.

What's more, this tactic can pay off in other ways.

By being open-minded and creative in your approach to pre-college programs, you may push your intellectual, physical and social boundaries, deepen your love of a particular area, or even explore a new field and find it incredibly fascinating.

And isn't that what college is all about?

The Benefits of Leveraging Professional Associations

A final smart way to locate pre-college programs of interest, and secure funding to attend one, is to go through professional associations.

Such searches can be very fruitful.

For example, let's say you're interested in journalism. You might discover JCamp, a six-day residential journalism program offered by the Asian American Journalists Association, which is free of charge to rising high school sophomores, juniors and seniors. (And no, you don't have to be Asian to qualify. There's no requirement to be an AAJA member either).

Those interested in medicine might consult the website of the Association of American Medical Colleges, which has a database list of summer programs in the medical field. This database resource helps students of all ages — from elementary students to undergraduates and graduate students — to locate enrichment programs on medical school campuses.

Another case in point: the American Mathematical Society maintains a list of summer programs, including several free and low-cost math camps.

Why are professional associations and career-related membership groups great places to find pre-college programs, especially affordable ones?

It's because they have a vested interested in students. They know the hurdles students will face academically, financially, socially and professionally. They've been there. And they want to help train and guide the next generation of future leaders in their respective industries. Many also want to give back simply because it's the right thing to do, or because they're grateful for their own success and the opportunities they've been afforded.

Some professional groups take a particular interest in supporting minorities, economically disadvantaged youth and under-represented students. They know the demographics of our society are changing. They realize that we are becoming an increasingly multi-cultural and global society. So these professional, industry and trade groups believe it is in the public's best interest to find and utilize all of our collective resources — human, financial, intellectual and otherwise — in order to prepare for the challenges of the next century.

Within these professional groups, as well as many undergraduate and graduate school programs, you can find "pipeline" programs that specifically target diverse students. These can be goldmines of opportunity for youth that possess academic and professional promise — along with the necessary passion, creativity, and initiative to help them stand out from the crowd.

How to Properly Capitalize on Pre-College Programs

I would be remiss in my duties if I merely ended the chapter here. So many people will urge you to attend a pre-college program as if simply listing the program on a resume were a magic passport of some kind, granting you easy access to the college or future of your dreams.

Obviously, that simply isn't true.

So let's talk about what is perhaps one of the most critical aspects of the pre-college program: what you do *during* and *after* the program ends.

The students who are most successful in capitalizing on pre-college experiences are those that do three things:

- Connect
- Contribute
- Communicate

Here's what each of these ideas entails, and how you can utilize each strategy to your benefit.

The Power of Making Personal Connections

We've all heard the expression: "it's not *what* you know, but *who* you know." It's a saying that basically means your personal connections are more important than your knowledge and skill set. The Chinese word for this concept is "guanxi" — which generally refers to one's personal relationships and other networks of influence.

I'll admit that I have mixed feelings about this concept.

At this point in my adult life, I'm wise enough to know that many people do indeed get ahead — or at least get a shot at their dreams — simply because of a personal or professional contact who pulled some strings, put in a good word, or just opened the right door.

Is this right? Is this fair? I'll leave that up to you to decide. But I think we all agree that it's reality. Even if you don't subscribe wholeheartedly to the belief that "it's *who* you know" that matters most, you probably can at least acknowledge that relationships do matter.

I also know from personal and professional experience, that "getting ahead" also requires hard work, talent — and knowledge. So it's not like you can completely skip the whole business of learning and acquiring skills, and purely rely on "*who* you know."

Given this reality — that it's beneficial to know your stuff *and* to know the "right" people — how should you utilize your time during a pre-college program?

I suggest that in addition to learning, taking the field trips, socializing and so on, that you take some time to strategically connect with key individuals.

Which individuals you choose to connect with really depends on your personal interests, goals and priorities.

For example, assume you hope to be a recruited athlete in football, but you're actually going to an academic pre-college program in Forensic Science because you love the whole CSI (Crime Scene Investigation) thing, and you're focused on that or criminal justice as a college major.

Well, naturally, you want to hit the books, study hard, and learn everything you can about forensic science during your pre-college program.

But also carve out some time during that stint to meet the head of the department, to personally introduce yourself to a professor whose work you've read about or whose dissertation or book you've read. You might also spend some time during office hours with a key researcher in the program simply learning about his or her background and what put that person on his or her career path.

By connecting with these people, you'll not only learn a lot more, you'll also make an impression on them and be more memorable than the countless mass of teens passing through these programs month after month and summer after summer.

And what about your sports interest? Don't you dare leave that campus without going to meet the football coach, talking to current players, and getting a more up-close and personal view of the football program. That will be far more insightful than simply taking a group tour, reading a brochure, or perusing information on the campus' website.

So in summary, you want to connect with key faculty, staff, coaches, students and any other individuals that may share an interest with you. These people may be tenured or adjunct professors, guest lecturers, outside speakers, admissions officials, financial aid personnel, department heads, student outreach officers, current freshmen, sophomores, juniors or seniors on campus, as well as other participants in the pre-college program, and more.

You never know how such relationships could develop down the road.

Needless to say, I'm not suggesting that you turn into a networking maniac and feel the need to "work the room" wherever you go. Just be yourself and try to make natural conversation with people (even if you're shy!) — and that's a really good start.

Why Students Must Contribute to the Program

While enrolled in a summer program, it's important to make a meaningful contribution.

What do you have to contribute? You can contribute in many ways: you can contribute to the larger campus, to the ongoing conversations in your group, and to the culture of the program.

The point is: Don't be a wallflower. Be assertive. Get in there, mix it up, and take advantage of opportunities presented to you, as well as the opportunities that arise to make an impact by sharing your time and talents. At the same time, stretch your boundaries and be willing to try new things. Don't be afraid to also share your personal story, your academic experiences, as well as inform people about your background or what drives and motivates you.

You probably do some of this already during the academic year. You may be contributing to your local community, to your school, or to various clubs in a host of ways. So figure out a way to make an impact on other participants in your pre-college program too.

One way to contribute is simply by being helpful. Perhaps you know a shortcut, a trick or a better way of doing something that others do not. Or maybe you notice another participant struggling to do or understand something, and you have the skills and the willingness to help that other person.

You may also help your cohorts by taking on a leadership role during group projects, study sessions, research, field activities or other pre-college program work.

In any group, there are many interpersonal and work dynamics. Sometimes, those with outgoing personalities or very strong verbal skills seem to naturally rise to the occasion, taking on leadership roles or becoming official or unofficial group leaders.

Even if you don't consider yourself a natural-born leader, or an assertive, "take-charge" kind of person, that shouldn't stop you from making a contribution. Your thoughts and ideas, your unique approach, your problem-solving skills and your input all matter. So no matter what your personality type, don't hesitate to pipe up and be heard.

You're in that pre-college program for a reason. Someone has already recognized that you belong there. So take advantage of all that the program has to offer — including an environment that fosters intellectual and social engagement. That's one key way you can make a contribution.

Even providing feedback to program directors and coordinators can be a way of making a meaningful contribution.

There's nothing to stop you from offering a program director some good ideas — some might say constructive criticism — to let him or her know what they could do to improve an offering.

It could be something as simple as recommending a course element that would be great to add or an excursion that could be improved in a certain way. Or perhaps you could offer your feedback on how to improve the program's mix of experiential learning (i.e. doing stuff) with the academic learning (via books, lectures, seminars and so on).

Pre-college officials and your peers will likely appreciate your input. Making suggestions for program improvements requires tact, of course. Don't bash any program or sound ungrateful for the opportunity to be there. Just approach it graciously, and say something like: "This has been a really rewarding program, and I have an idea I'd like to share on how to make it even better."

The Essential Final Ingredient: Communication

The final step in making your pre-college program experience a true success is in communicating with others after the program ends.

Ideally, your communication will come in verbal and written form.

For starters, do send a thank you note to the program head, letting him or her know that you appreciated the time spent there.

You can also share what you learned and what you gained from the experience.

And remember all those people you met during the program as well? Now is the time to follow-up with them. Do it soon after you return home, while the memories are still fresh in your mind.

Very often, when teens meet others students (and adults) during pre-college programs, they promise to keep in touch — but then everyone gets busy and life gets in the way. So the individuals you reach out to will appreciate your diligence and follow-through.

Perhaps most importantly, however, you need to be able to convey to others — people who weren't at your pre-college program — how the experience benefited you.

Let's say you have a college interview. If an admissions officer or a college alum asks you about your pre-college program, you should be able to clearly articulate the importance of the experience and explain how it helped to prepare you for college, expand your knowledge about something, or maybe brought new revelations.

Doing this effectively will require some reflection on your part. It's not simply enough to run down a laundry list of pre-college program activities. The important thing to explain is: what were your personal takeaways from those activities? How did the program help you to learn and grow?

For those who are into journaling (and even those who aren't), writing down your day's activities, academic or personal lessons learned, and other insights as they come to you, preferably while you're enrolled in the program, will be helpful in later remembering the breadth of your pre-college experience.

But since there's often little to no down-time during many pre-college programs, even just jotting down a few notes about special highlights is advisable each day or every few days. You can also do this after the fact, if you absolutely can't squeeze it in during the program.

It's also possible that you may later use some of those notes to explain — in a college essay or a scholarship application — some key part of your pre-college experience.

Again, communication about your pre-collegiate event is a critically important component of the entire experience. So be careful not to neglect this vital aspect.

By now you have a really good sense of the breadth of opportunities available to you in the realm of pre-college programs. And hopefully, you also fully understand that you don't have to go broke trying to pay for these pre-collegiate experiences.

But what if you decide to forgo pre-college programs altogether? Despite what you make think, that's perfectly fine!

You have plenty of options to stay busy in the summer and still partake in meaningful activities that can help you develop personally and academically, shine in your pursuit of college admissions — and even make it more feasible to nab college scholarships, too.

CHAPTER 6

FREE SUMMER ACTIVITIES FOR COLLEGE-BOUND STUDENTS

As previously mentioned, pre-college programs aren't the only outlets to turbo-charge your summer activities while in high school. You can also do the following:

- Volunteer Your Services
- Do an Internship
- Get a Job
- Engage in Distance Learning
- Conduct Independent Study

Volunteer Your Services

Doing volunteer work, over the summer or even during the course of the school year, is a great way to make an impact in your local community, help others in need, and even learn valuable skills.

Equally important, volunteering is a no-cost way to stay productive, engaged and true to yourself if you find the right organization or effort to support.

When you think about volunteer activities, the first thing that probably springs to your mind is performing various hands-on activities tied directly to a social cause.

Perhaps you picture yourself (or others) cooking for and feeding the homeless, taking clothes and donated toys to orphaned kids, or visiting elderly residents at a senior citizens center.

Those are all wonderful things to do. But what if you don't particularly have an interest in those things or similar "do-gooder" causes? Realize that you're not alone; not everyone has a burning desire to save the whales or develop freshwater solutions for drought-prone areas of the world.

If this sounds like you, let me say right off the top that you shouldn't try to drum up a laundry list of random service activities just to slap "volunteer work" on your resume. College admission officers can see right through that.

It's great to have a passion for community service, and for some people it just seems to come naturally. However, don't beat yourself up because you're really not that interested in typical volunteer work, or because it seems like other students are out there on the front lines doing highly visible volunteer activities like running for a cancer cure or rescuing abused pets.

Again, if that's where your heart is, go for it! But if you can't quite muster up the desire to do something like that day after day, or week after week, realize that you do have alternatives.

First, think about the kind of individual you truly are. Do you consider yourself an indoor or an outdoor kind of person? Also, do you like to work solo, engage with others one-on-one, or take part in activities involving large groups?

Next, evaluate the things you really enjoy doing. Maybe you just like to read all day in your spare time, or you'd be quite content to fool around with computers for hours on end. Or perhaps your ideal day is spent outdoors, enjoying nice weather and mixing and mingling with people every now and again.

Well, there are plenty of organizations and people who could benefit from all those things.

You could read to elementary school kids, or go to a disadvantaged youth program, introducing kids there to some books they may not know and giving them a greater appreciation of language arts and literacy. Such efforts on your part would bolster their reading and writing skills, too.

Here's another alternative for computer savvy types. N...ganizations of every kind can only thrive when they have a healthy list or donors. So you could set up and manage a computer database that tracks a non-profit's donors. Or you could use your computer skills to do a ton of other important activities, like:

- Build a charity's website or blog
- Help a non-profit launch an online crowd-funding campaign
- Create a spreadsheet to itemize an organization's expenses
- Perform back-engine work lets the group keeps better tabs on clients served

The possibilities are endless. So how do you know which non-profit to pick or where to start?

Just select any number of groups by checking out websites like AllForGood.org or VolunteerMatch.org, both of which pair good causes with people willing to help those efforts. The latter site even has thousands of virtual volunteer opportunities, which you can do from home or anywhere, just by logging onto your computer!

And what about those of you who like to be outdoors, yet don't want to feel lost in a big crowd? Something as simple as going door-to-door to get petitions signed or to raise awareness about an important issue could suit you perfectly.

I hope you get my point — which is that volunteerism can be whatever you make it, and there's no shame in having it align nicely with your own personal interests and preferences. In the end, you'll be making a difference, and you'll probably wind up learning a lot about yourself as well.

Plus, here's one more insight about volunteering that no one probably ever shared with you. Some of you might initially think: "there's nothing I'm really *passionate* about." Don't let that dissuade you or cause you to not take action. Be willing to stretch a bit and go beyond your comfort zone if necessary. Chances are, you'll find the volunteer work you performed was way more rewarding than you ever imagined it would be.

Just remember: non-profit groups live and die based not just on the monies they collect to carry out their mission, but also based on the enormous efforts of hard-working and willing volunteers.

That's why Martin Luther King Jr. once said: *"Everybody can be great because everybody can serve."*

In the end, volunteering just might be one of the extra things that makes *you* great.

Do an Internship

Speaking of challenging yourself, what's to stop you from getting a summer internship as a totally new challenge? It could be an internship related to a career you may be interested in pursuing or connected to a major or minor you're thinking of declaring in college.

Or it could be an internship that forces you to undertake new projects, assignments, experiences or other activities that are completely "not like you."

Maybe there's something that you've always wanted to try or just something that doesn't really fit with your current view of yourself. Are you the artsy type who has never been into athletics? Why not try your hand at a sport (any sport!) over the summer — even recreationally — and see how you like it.

Or maybe you're a science and math geek through and through (and I mean that in a good way!), but you've never learned much about ancient literature or modern film-making techniques. Could you be persuaded to do something totally different, just for the sake or learning and having a unique summer experience?

Whatever the case, interning can give you a bird's eye view into any number of careers or industries, not to mention help you land valuable contacts that might hire you later.

You'll get to see how an organization operates from the ground up, get exposed to key aspects of a specific occupation, and understand the work culture of a company, government agency or non-profit.

Internships also offer the possibility to get paid, though most high-school age interns don't earn money. Still, by interning over the summer, you or your family won't be spending money, either.

Get a Job

Working for a few weeks or a few months is another worthwhile — and under-rated — way to pass the summer. A job is also a summer activity that can put dollars into your pocket, as opposed to pre-college programs, which can take dollars out of your wallet or your parents' bank account.

Some of you may hold down part-time jobs during the academic year, so the thought of working is nothing new to you.

But for those who haven't yet began working for pay, know that virtually any type of job you obtain will give you valuable experience.

Sure, some jobs are higher paying than others, and some positions may have a higher perceived "prestige" value among your buddies. But don't think for a moment that colleges will look askance at you just because you spent a summer flipping burgers, selling clothes in a retail store, or working as a lifeguard. I wouldn't necessarily recommend you do that for all four summers of your high school career. But believe me when I say that admission officers will recognize that you're not a goof-off if you can hold down a job for several months or even several years.

Being continuously employed means you likely took the initiative to go find work, got up every morning (or even each afternoon) to get to work on time, interacted successfully with co-workers and customers, and learned about the duties and responsibilities of your particular position. That's pretty impressive for a teenager.

Plus, given economic realities and the cost of college today, admission officials do understand that many students really *need* to work.

"It doesn't concern me in the slightest that you didn't go to France or that you didn't have a Washington internship over the summer," says Whitman Smith, director of admissions at the University of Mississippi. In fact, he thinks it's good for families to "have students incur some of the cost of their higher education, especially by working in the summer."

There's one other bonus to getting a 9-to-5.

Working can promote your overall maturity, which is a boon to college preparedness. Colleges want to enroll mature, responsible young adults who are ready for the next phase of life. What better way to demonstrate maturity than being a responsible, hard-working employee?

Says Karen Richardson, from Tufts University: "If you worked in the grocery store, which is what I did before I went to college (at Princeton), and you learned from it, then that's perfectly fine."

"Students also shouldn't think that they need to have a pricey pre-college experience where they're trying to save the world," Richardson adds.

"They may have spent a summer babysitting. As long as they can articulate what that experience taught them, that's what counts. It's really about the voice of the applicant coming through — not what a student did, but how they talk about what they learned."

Engage in Distance Learning or Conduct Independent Study

Distance learning and independent study are two final activities that can be readily accomplished during the summer months (or year-round) as pre-college activities.

These two options, though, are best utilized by high-achieving students, focused teens or curious learners who don't necessarily need a lot of hand-holding and guidance from instructors or parents.

In fact, students who have the richest distance learning experiences and independent study projects are typically those with a craving to explore new topics, or delve deeper into subjects about which they're already passionate.

Distance learning programs are plentiful and can be found online for nearly any subject under the sun. And don't think that online programs are too pricey, boring or lacking in academic rigor. Rest assured that you can find cost-free, exciting distance learning options at a range of colleges — even among Ivy League schools and other top-tier institutions.

Free Online Learning Options At Penn, MIT and Harvard

Let's say you want to learn about marketing. The University of Pennsylvania's Wharton School has a free online learning program known as Knowledge@ Wharton High School, or KWHS.

You can spend an entire summer online at KWHS, learning The Foundations of Marketing, and gaining knowledge about everything from branding and consumer behavior to strategy and the 5 P's of marketing (product, price, placement, packaging, and promotion).

But if tackling marketing alone isn't enough to keep you busy, there's a lot more where that came from.

According to the website, Penn's KWHS worked with high school students, educators, Wharton students and business professionals to develop over 400 lesson plans that cover 10 subjects: Accounting, Career Development, Communication, Computation, Economics, Entrepreneurship, International Business, Management, Marketing and Personal Finance.

If marketing isn't your thing because you're more of a math and technology person, think about applying to MOSTEC, the MIT Online Science, Technology and Engineering Community.

In a recent program, running from July 2014 to January 2015, scholars accepted into the MITES program engaged in an online community, interacting with faculty and staff at MIT. These high-school standouts didn't just expand their knowledge about science and engineering, they also got pointers about college admissions and financial aid. As a nice bonus, students could complete projects and then present their work, in person, during a five-day conference at MIT.

Even Harvard offers distance education classes, via the Harvard Extension School. In total, there are more than 200 Harvard online classes, letting students take a Harvard course from anywhere across the globe.

Courses can be found online through video, and can be played back on demand. These feature Harvard faculty giving past lectures.

Separately, you can also view Harvard classes in real-time, either via online video or live web-conference format. Some of these classes also include weekend lectures on campus. (But these online courses take place in the fall and spring semesters, and they include regularly scheduled homework assignments and exams).

Independent study can be accomplished in a variety of ways: by working on a completely solo basis, via a distance-learning program, and even by working with professional mentors, high school teachers or professors at local colleges and universities.

To work with a professor, you'll have to take the initiative to reach out to him or her, articulate your area of interest, and arrange for some academic oversight to help you explore and deepen your knowledge of the subject in question.

Depending on your academic work and individual school policy, you may or may not get high school or college credit for independent study undertaken as a high school student.

But the prospect of being able to learn something new, do research, or further explore a topic that has piqued your curiosity could be a priceless, productive way to spend your summer.

The Importance of Documenting Your Summer Activities

Regardless of whether you enroll in an academic pre-college program, do volunteer work, land an internship, get a job, or decide on a distance learning or an independent study project, you'd be wise to document your summer activities.

It's easy enough to add certain things to your resume, like campus clubs you've joined or leadership roles you may have assumed in student government.

But don't forget to track those accomplishments and less formal activities that take place during the summer. You can put those items on a resume, of course. But even if you don't put them on your resume, be sure to write down (for yourself) what the experience taught you and how it benefited you. (Remember my advice in the previous chapter about what you should be doing *during* and *after* a pre-college program ends? The same suggestions apply here).

Writing things down will help you to later recall how you spent your time, what insights you gained, and more. This can also be helpful for scholarships and even your job prospects down the road.

Let's say you decided to do some volunteer work with an environmental group, or you conducted your own survey about air contamination in town. Maybe you went to public meetings, polled your neighbors, or researched the impact of pollution in your local area. Who knows? But your ability to document any lessons learned or any positive outcomes achieved will be favorably viewed, not just by colleges, but also by future employers.

An interesting LinkedIn survey, found that 41% of employers said they consider volunteer work equally as valuable as paid work experience when they are screening job candidates. Also, 20% of hiring managers surveyed said they have made a hiring decision based on a candidate's volunteer work experience.

College Secret:

Many employers say your volunteer work is just as important as paid work experience. So even if you've never had a part-time or full-time job, your charitable activities can give you an edge when job hunting.

In addition to potentially boosting your academic and professional credentials, some of your summer activities may simply help you grow as a person, get up to date on current affairs, get more comfortable writing business correspondences, or maybe more prepared to tackle some other topic you'll need to master in college.

Some of you may be able to create a portfolio of sorts showing your work in action. You may have photos, newspaper articles, thank you letters and other items that highlight your work or achievements. Keep these — or even hand them off to Mom, if she's well organized and would love to put together a scrapbook of your activities.

I created an "Important Documents" binder for all three of my children and it has proven invaluable, allowing me — at a moment's notice — to put my hands on everything from year-end grades and academic transcripts to honors and awards my children have earned.

When it came time for my oldest daughter to put together her first resume, during her sophomore year of high school, our binder was a Godsend as it reminded her of all the things she'd done and accomplished.

You can and should do the same thing to properly document your summer activities, as well as the year-round activities that make you the unique person you are.

CAMPUS TOURS AND COLLEGE VISITS

Campus tours and college visits have always been, to a greater or lesser degree, an important aspect of the higher education selection process.

But a generation ago, college-bound youth often applied to colleges and universities without ever having actually visited their selected institutions. Back then, many teenagers simply picked the schools of their choice, submitted applications to these campuses, and showed up right before classes started. This was true regardless of whether the college was 200 or 2,000 miles away from home.

Not everyone did it this way, however, and many students from decades past also took to the road, physically visiting the campuses of their choice.

Today, thanks to a host of factors — such as increased technology, the growth of social media, and stepped-up college recruitment activity — students have more opportunities than ever to not only physically visit post-secondary schools, but to also conduct online tours from the comfort and convenience of their own homes.

Whether you plan to do in-person visits or Web-based tours, it's critical to find out all that an institution has to offer to know whether the school will meet your academic, social, and financial needs.

Campus tours and information sessions can provide you with an admissions edge as well. That's because many colleges and universities look to see whether an applicant has shown "demonstrated interest" in attending the institution. And an in-person campus visit is one way to show that you're seriously considering the school.

If you haven't made any contact at all with a school, and then you later apply, you're considered a "ghost" applicant. That's not good. College officials might assume you're only applying as a "backup" and that you're not really interested in that institution. School visits are so important that many colleges and universities use them, to greater or lesser degrees, in evaluating your admissions application. For example, the website of Holy Cross notes:

> *"At Holy Cross, a student's contact with our office is monitored. Every time a student interacts with our office, we note it in their file because we feel that those interactions serve not only to better acquaint the student with our school, but also demonstrate (to some extent) the level of interest that student has in Holy Cross. If students are able to travel to campus for a visit, they should do so and make sure to sign in with our front desk."*

But what if you live all the way across country, or even just in an adjacent state, and it would be a financial hardship to travel to a school or to multiple schools? Well, fortunately, there are ways to complete campus tours and visits without breaking the bank.

Seven Strategies To Reduce Your Costs

This chapter will cover seven strategies you can use to reduce — or even completely eliminate — the cost of campus tours and visits.

The seven strategies are:

1. Do a "virtual" college tour
2. Attend online and regional college fairs
3. Get free college visits through "Fall Fly-Ins"
4. Take advantage of free "Spring Fly-Ins"
5. Compare a group vs. individual tour
6. Plan ahead to save time, money and effort
7. Get reimbursements, college credit and other perks

Here's a look at each and what you need to know about touring campus colleges that are near and far.

When funds are especially limited, and you know there's no possible way to take a long-distance trip to a distant college, realize that you do have other ways to glean insights into a campus, including its culture.

Two strategies in particular will be beneficial, at least preliminarily, for cash-strapped students wanting to conduct college visits.

Strategy #1: Do a "Virtual" College Tour

Many colleges and universities offer "virtual" campus tours, using Web-based platforms to help students and their families "see" a campus online.

Internet college tours were first introduced in the late 1990s, but really didn't take off until a decade or so later. In the past five years, virtual campus tours have surged in popularity, largely as a way to address tighter family budgets and to help colleges expand their marketing and outreach efforts.

To find out whether a campus you're interested in offers a virtual tour — and many do — you can simply go to the school's website and search the section for visitors or prospective students. You will often find what you're looking for in areas labeled something like: "Visit Us," "Schedule a Tour" or "Take a Virtual Tour."

Alternatively, you can go to a number of websites that aggregate virtual tours, allowing you to view a large number of different online campus tours in one location.

In 1997, a Florida-based company called YOUniversityTV created the first College Video Resource Community. Students can now visit YOUniversityTV.com and see video campus tours of more than 400 colleges across the country.

CampusTours.com is another popular site that has videos of more than 1,200 campuses. Campus Tours, based in Maine, is an interactive media and software company that specializes in developing virtual tours, video tours, and interactive maps.

YouVisit is a third well-known company that creates virtual walking tours for colleges and universities. It too has hundreds of online tours you can peruse from your desktop, laptop or even your mobile device.

In 2011, Google tiptoed into the business of taking college searches virtual. By 2014, dozens of brand-name colleges nationwide were using

Google tools, such as video chats, to help connect students virtually to their campuses. Among these tools are Google Hangouts, a multi-person video chat platform, and Google+ Hangouts On Air, which are publicly streamed Google Hangouts that allow anyone to watch.

When Duke University officials teamed up with Google in 2012, turnout for the very first Hangouts was high as students clamored to learn more about Duke. Since then, interest from students has only grown — for group information sessions and for one-on-one chats via Hangouts as well.

"We saw Google Hangouts and Hangouts on Air as a way to connect current students to admitted students so they could really see themselves as part of the Duke experience," says Cara Rousseau, social media manager at Duke University.

Rousseau adds that virtual platforms also help with international recruitment.

"International students may not have the resources to make an in-person visit," Rousseau notes. "So these virtual tools bring our global audience to us."

For example, because China places restrictions on various forms of social media, Duke reaches prospective Chinese students through Renren, which has been dubbed the Chinese version of Facebook, and through Sina Wei Bo, which is the equivalent of Twitter in China.

Those are just some of the ways Duke is ramping up its social networking activities in response to favorable feedback from students and their parents.

In 2014, the school also created a private Facebook group for the parents of admitted students to connect with parents of current students who come from various backgrounds, geographic locations and viewpoints.

"That parent group was very, very talkative — more active than the student group," Rousseau says. "We really feel like it gives parents a sense of stability and better insights, instead of just talking to an admissions officer, because other parents provide an unguarded perspective and really speak candidly about their family's experience."

The school's Google Hangouts have expanded as well.

Each April, Duke now holds four or five Hangouts for newly admitted students who are weighing their college options.

"The first Hangout is always most popular and typically gets over 1,000 participants. Since our freshman class is usually around 1,700 students, that's a large percentage of students participating," Rousseau notes.

The Hangouts highlight various themes — such as academics, arts and humanities, student life, dining, global education and studying abroad — to give prospective students a taste of Duke's culture. Videos are also shot in a wide variety of locations, showing school pride and spirit, from the athletics stadium to the Duke Lemur Center.

So what can you expect when you take a virtual campus tour?

You can actually learn a lot, as virtual college tours can provide prospective students and their families with highlights of any of the following:

- Academic facilities, including classrooms, lecture halls and libraries
- Athletic centers and recreational amenities
- College clubs and student activities
- Open spaces, especially outdoor courtyards or quadrangles (i.e. "quads"), lush gardens, and sweeping college lawns
- Public spaces or services, like dining halls, restaurants or student centers
- Student housing, such as dorm rooms, apartments and residence halls

Besides showing you physical buildings and special sights on campus, many virtual college tours try to convey a sense of campus life and the overall flavor of the school. This is done through interviews with students, vignettes showing college traditions, and sometimes even interactive features that let you learn more about an area of interest on campus.

All of these things can help you get an initial sense of whether you'd enjoy living and learning at a particular college campus.

But educators caution that virtual tours aren't meant to replace in-person visits.

"Anecdotally, it seems like visits to campus are not declining at all, especially during busy times, like spring break and over the summer," says Duke's Rousseau. "Virtual tours enhance the visitor experience because these online tools just give people more ways to learn about a school."

Still, for budget-conscious students and families, an online tour is a must — at least as a starting point.

Since most four-year colleges now use social media to foster communication with students, when you're trying to experience colleges from afar, it's also helpful to go to their Facebook, Twitter, Instagram, Pinterest and Spotify pages. You can see if they have Google Plus accounts or YouTube channels as well.

Data about campus tour activity suggest that students are now taking more physical and online tours, and that the two are not mutually exclusive.

A recent Google study revealed that 90% of students use the Internet to research higher education institutions. YouVisit reports that about 80% of applicants will physically visit no more than four college campuses.

It's no surprise, then, that the number of students taking virtual tours has spiked dramatically over the past five years. Yet some college officials say the numbers of students participating in on-site visits are up as well, in part from students who have first taken a virtual college tour.

Baylor in 2013 unveiled a series of "Guided Virtual Tours" that give you — quite literally — a bird's-eye perspective of the campus. The tours are comprised of four videos, all narrated by different Baylor students. While it's not particularly unique to feature students in campus videos, what is unique is that the videos were all shot from a helicopter, providing one-of-a-kind, breathtaking views of the entire campus.

The result is that this virtual tour not only nicely captures the spirit of Baylor — from dorm life and campus traditions to academics and study abroad opportunities — it also showcases Baylor's beauty, including The Baylor Marina, The Rock, and the Bill and Eva Williams Bear Habitat.

Even an in-person visit wouldn't capture those things — at least not from the vantage point of being anywhere from 20 feet to several thousand feet above ground.

Strategy #2: Attend Online and Regional College Fairs

In addition to conducting online college tours, another free way to "visit" with a campus — or its representatives — is to attend online college fairs and regional, in-person college events too.

Cappex, a free site that lets you search for colleges, financial aid and scholarships, puts on the CappexConnect Online College Fair each year. It consistently draws admission officers and financial aid representatives from nearly 100 good schools around the country. These officials give live presentations to help you better navigate your entrance into higher education.

CollegeWeekLive is another live, online event that connects students at no charge to representatives from approximately 300 colleges and universities. The site hosts individual online college information sessions, and college fairs on an ongoing basis.

But if you can't leave your region or state for college visits, you do have other alternatives beyond those found online.

Every year, the National Association for College Admission Counseling (NACAC) and its regional affiliates conduct the largest college fairs in America.

NACAC holds spring and fall events, dubbed National College Fairs, in every state in the U.S.

In addition to these general interest college fairs, NACAC also conducts Performing and Visual Arts College Fairs twice a year.

Students and their families can attend these fairs at no charge and gain a wealth of information on hundreds of colleges and universities.

By attending an NACAC college fair, you can learn all about your target schools, connect with university representatives, and get on their radar to let them know of your interest in specific programs.

Among college fair options, you can also take advantage of college consortium presentations. These are joint presentations that colleges and universities (usually those of similar caliber) conduct together, live and in-person.

One such consortium is the "Exploring College Options Consortium" comprising admission officers from Duke, Georgetown, Harvard, Penn and Stanford.

You might wonder why an elite school like Harvard, for example, would team up with a cross-country rival like Stanford to do information sessions in different areas nationwide.

It's because many prestigious schools engage in what I call "co-opetition" with one another in the realm of college recruitment. These highly selective colleges are typically seeking students from the same talent pool — high achievers, diverse kids with great grades and test scores, standout student athletes, as well as college-bound students with special skills and abilities.

These colleges know that they "compete" with each other for students' attention, but they also "cooperate" with one another (i.e. "co-opetition") because it's often more cost effective and efficient to work in tandem. By teaming up on neutral ground — often at hotels, convention centers or other large venues — they can better draw large numbers of students to these college information sessions. Needless to say, joint presentations are also more attractive to students hoping to cut down on the high costs associated with travelling to individual schools.

Another big consortium you can attend, without having to travel far, is the free Exploring Education Excellence event. It's a series of in-person info sessions designed for students, families and school counselors interested in getting more information about Brown, University of Chicago, Cornell, Columbia, and Rice University.

At various college consortium fairs, there are both introductory presentations from each individual campus, as well as Q&A sessions where you can ask representatives from any school specific questions about the college search process, admissions, financial aid and more.

Additionally, don't forget about local college fairs, open houses and informational events that may be held right on the campuses of postsecondary schools located in or near your town, city or region.

Besides serving as an informational resource, college fairs offer another possible perk to would-be students: the potential to be *instantly* granted admission to a given college. About 25% of U.S. colleges and universities offer on-the-spot admission to prospective students at college fairs, high school visits, as well as on-campus events, according to the National Association for College Admission Counseling. The practice is far more widespread at public colleges than private institutions, and it's typically done at less selective colleges. Still, it's something to keep in mind if you attend a college fair.

The Secrets to Taking In-Person College Tours for Little-to-No Cash

So far, we've talked about two primary ways (virtual tours and college fairs) to make campus visits and get information about colleges without ever having to spend money or even leave your local area.

Let's turn now to some advice that will make it possible for you to physically visit your dream college, either completely free or at a greatly reduced expense.

Strategy #3: Get Free College Visits Through "Fall Fly-in

Like most aspects of higher education, campus tours and visits can carry a hefty price tag. But that doesn't mean these trips have to be paid on *your* dime.

Did you know that before you even apply to some schools, there's a little-known way to see those campuses in-person completely free — courtesy of the colleges or universities themselves?

College Secret:

You can take all-expense paid trips to visit various colleges and universities — if you know which schools to target and how to get them to invite you.

During these trips, most of which take place in the fall, the school will take care of your round-trip transportation costs, such as your train or airline ticket. Likewise, the institution will cover your lodging for a few days, and will even pay for your meals while you're there.

Sounds like a great deal, right? It is! You just have to do some basic research, find out whether you qualify, and then fill out an application for something known as a college "fly-in program."

Since these programs are designed to let you briefly experience residential life at a college or university, they often pack a lot of activities into a two- or three-day stay. During a fly-in program, you might:

- Attend a sports event
- Eat in a student dining hall
- Have an interview with an admissions officer
- Learn about financial aid the school offers
- Meet one or more professors
- Participate in academic or career-oriented workshops
- See the local town or city and nearby sites of interest
- Sit in on a class of your choice
- Socialize with current students

- Spend a night or more in a dorm
- Take a campus tour
- Use college or university facilities, like libraries and athletic centers
- Visit multicultural centers or diverse clubs on campus

Again, the idea is to give you a crash course into campus life to let you discover if you like the campus and would find it a nice place to call home while you're a college student.

So where can these great "Fall Fly-Ins" be found?

Highly selective, private schools represent the majority of institutions offering paid-for visits *before* students actually apply. And while most campuses offering fly-Ins are liberal arts colleges, many types of schools host these events.

Some of these institutions include: Amherst, Barnard, Bates, Bowdoin, Brandeis, Bryn Mawr, Carleton, Colby, Colegate, College of Charleston, Connecticut College, Dartmouth, Davidson, Franklin & Marshall, Harvey Mudd, Kalamazoo College, MIT, Miami University, Macalester, Oberlin, Pitzer, Reed College, Scripps, Sewanee, Simpson College, Swarthmore, Tufts, Wellesley and Whitman College.

Many more private schools, as well as top public schools, also offer free campus trips *after* students are admitted. But those visits differ in several ways, and I'll give you the skinny on that shortly.

At this point, though, let me explain who is eligible for a free, upfront campus visit and how you can secure one of these incredibly beneficial trips.

Diversity and Inclusion Reign

The vast majority of all-expense-paid campus visits come through recruitment drives for targeted high school seniors, and sometimes juniors. In most cases, the students being targeted are racial and ethnic minorities; low-income students or teens from varying socio-economic classes; youth from all backgrounds whose parents did not earn a four-year degree; and under-represented members in various fields, such as females in STEM programs or students with learning disabilities.

But it's important to realize that these programs are often quite competitive, just like regular college admissions. It's not enough to simply check off a box indicating: "I'm Black," "I'm Hispanic" or "I'm a first generation college student." It doesn't work that way.

For starters, two thirds of all higher education institutions (67%) do not use race as a factor in the admission decision.

At the same time, college officials certainly want to promote diversity and foster inclusiveness. They also want to find and reward two categories of students — academic standouts who have already excelled; and very promising, good-to-great students who want to push themselves intellectually despite limited resources or other obstacles they may face.

Once you locate a Fall Fly-In of interest, getting in isn't just about your personal and academic background. Depending on the campus, you will also have to do some work in the application process.

Colleges and universities offering Fly-In programs have different application guidelines and processes. But you usually have to complete an application, write an essay, submit academic transcripts and provide ACT, PSAT, or SAT test scores.

A few programs require that a teacher or counselor nominate you or provide a letter of recommendation on your behalf. However, certain colleges may reach out to you directly, sending you an email or a letter inviting you to apply. This usually happens if a high school counselor refers you to a college, or if a college buys lists of names of students who have tested well on standardized college exams.

When a Fly-In program requires you to be nominated, that nomination doesn't always have to come from someone at your high school. An official from a college access program can also nominate you, providing a pathway to free college visits.

For instance, QuestBridge College Prep Scholars are nominated for all-expense-paid college visits, and the QuestBridge program typically awards 100 to 200 students with a free campus visit. The College Prep Scholarship application is usually due in March.

As you can see, seeking entrance into a Fall Fly-In program is sort of an earlier mini-version of the overall college application process.

Why is it so involved?

Schools that sponsor Fly-In initiatives are devoting a lot of time and resources to these efforts — and the candidates they choose. So they want to be sure to only select individuals with genuine interest in the campus, as well as:

a. Students that meet the school's program goals
b. Academically serious teens that truly merit the wonderful opportunity that a fly-in program provides.

When you're hunting for these opportunities, realize that each college offering paid campus trips may call its program by a different name or a specific moniker. For instance, Oberlin picks up the tab for high-achieving students of color visiting the campus via its MVP or Multicultural Visit Program. Meanwhile, Amherst hosts two weekend Diversity Open Houses for which students of all backgrounds are welcome to apply.

Regardless of their names, this kind of freebie trip is generally referred to as a "Campus Fly-In," a "Diversity Fly-In," or a "Diversity Open House."

At Tufts, their annual Fall Fly-In Program is called "The Voices of Tufts Diversity Experience."

"It's an overnight program for senior high school students, and we do require an application, a short essay about why they'd like to attend, a transcript and a letter of recommendation from a guidance counselor," says Tufts' Karen Richardson.

"We get well over 500 applications and about 250 to 270 students come from all across the country. If it's a financial hardship for them to come, we fly them in or pay for their train fare," she says.

During the program, students pack in a lot — and come away with a lot, too. They sit in on classes, attend separate Q&A panels with students and the Dean of Admission, spend the night in a dorm, and view campus clubs and performances in action.

Equally important, Tufts facilitates small group sessions of 10 to 12 students "so we as admissions counselors can get to know students better," Richardson says. At the end of the program, there's an admissions workshop to tell students how to make their applications stand out from the pack.

"With the Voices program, if we have 250 students come, over 200 end up applying for admission to Tufts," says Richardson. "It traditionally attracts students of color and LGBT students, but anyone who's interested in learning more about diversity on the Tufts campus is welcome to apply."

* * *

In the summer before her senior year of high school and right when the schoolyear began, my oldest daughter received more than a dozen Fly-In offers from top schools all across the country, including Scripps, Hamilton, Tufts, Wellesley, Davidson, MIT, Emory, the University of Pennsylvania, the University of Miami at Oxford and more.

I suspect her very strong PSAT and SAT scores (which colleges can acquire through the College Board) put her on the radar of many elite schools.

But those Fly-In invitations likewise made her consider several institutions that previously were not on *her* radar. As parent, I was glad to see my daughter broaden her collegiate options. I was also grateful to know that I wouldn't have to personally fund these potential college visits.

Besides helping you to save hundreds or possibly thousands of dollars in travel costs, Fly-In programs boast another huge benefit.

Some students (and even certain school officials) say that if you attend one of these programs, you increase your chances of winning admission into the same school.

However, don't worry if you apply for a Fly-In program and don't get accepted.

I know this may sound contradictory. But college admission officers say that not getting into a Fly-In program doesn't *negatively* impact your actual college admission application at all.

After all, many students get turned down for Fly-In programs for reasons well beyond their academic credentials and student profiles.

It could be something as simple as geographic preference. Perhaps the school is actively looking for students in a certain section of the country and it happens to be where you don't live. It may also be the case that the school where you want a Fly-In is assessing applicants in various ways, giving higher priority to students with severe financial difficulties or those from specific racial groups.

And finally, a denial to a Fly-In program could be nothing more than sheer numbers. Colleges don't have unlimited budgets. So the truth is that funding for programs like these is limited and will only cover a specific number of students, usually anywhere from 20 to a maximum of 200 or so students per program.

Despite those statistics, realize that Fly-In programs can help lead to some other important numbers: major dollars for college.

Miami University of Ohio has a diversity fly-in program called Bridges that not only gives free travel, but also guarantees that if students complete the program, are later admitted, and then enroll at the campus, they'll receive $10,000 to $16,000 in scholarship money. These funds, $2,500 to $4,000 annually for four years, are only awarded to Bridges students. Additionally, 10 Bridges students are selected to receive full tuition scholarships for their four years of study at Miami University's Oxford campus. That makes this fly-in program worth more than $110,000 for successful out-of-state students.

To find out if the schools on your college list have Fly-In programs, go to CollegeMapper.com, click on the "Colleges" menu," and then select the "Diversity Support Programs" tab. There you can select a filter labeled "Open House/Fly In." If a college or university has a Fly-In program, it should be listed there.

The website GetMeToCollege.org also maintains a list of colleges that offer free campus visits.

Strategy #4: Take Advantage of Free "Spring Fly-Ins"

If finances prevent you from visiting a distant campus on your own, and you don't get accepted into a Fly-In program *before* submitting your college application, you can always wait until *after* you've applied to a school, and then attend another type of free Fly-In.

Just like colleges and universities fund "Fall Fly-In" programs, certain institutions also offer all-expense-paid campus visits that take place in the spring and target diverse students either *after* they've applied or *after* they've been accepted.

These free trips are called "Spring Fly-Ins."

There are relative advantages and disadvantages to attending a "Spring Fly-In" versus a "Fall Fly-In."

For starters, going to see a school in the fall gives you a chance to know whether you truly want to apply to a given campus or not. You also get the opportunity to broaden the potential mix of colleges and universities on your list.

Perhaps you may not normally have considered, for example, certain schools in New England, California or the Midwest. But you might have a very positive Fall Fly-In experience and become totally smitten with a campus in any of those locations. So the earlier a Fly-In program takes place, the broader your options.

For timing reasons, though, you might prefer one type of Fly-In as opposed to the other.

Fall Fly-Ins can take place anytime between September and December. But many campuses try to schedule Fall-Fly Ins in the months of October and November. In fact, some arrange for these events around federal holidays, like Columbus Day, which is the second Monday in October, or Veterans Day, which falls on November 11. Presumably, colleges and universities do that in the hopes that you won't have to miss too much school to attend.

Depending on your schedule, a Fall Fly-In may work perfectly for you, or it may not work at all — especially if you're studying for a first or repeat sitting of the ACT or SAT.

Similarly, a Spring Fly-In that takes place in March or April may be awesome for your schedule, or it could be ill-timed if it interferes with sports, extra-curricular activities or school exams you're scheduled to take.

From a programming and activities standpoint, Fall and Spring Fly-Ins are quite similar. However, some people say that spring programs are even more attractive affairs because certain schools really roll out the red carpet treatment to impress you during these events.

Why is that?

Some schools may be more enamored of Spring Fly-In students for a few reasons.

First, since you've gone through the extra step of *applying* to the campus for freshman admission, you've clearly indicated demonstrated interest in that college or university.

By contrast, with most Fall Fly-Ins, selected students can do these free visits and later decide not to apply to a campus because they are under no obligation to do so. As a practical matter, many Fall Fly-In students will in fact apply. But submitting an application for college admission is not a requirement for the vast majority of Fall Fly-Ins.

There's another reason schools may have greater interest in you during a Spring Fly-In. If admissions decisions have been made or are close to being finalized, which usually happens in the month of March, a school can know with greater certainty that it wants you. The only question that remains is: do you likewise want to attend that particular school? In fact, many schools offer Spring Fly-Ins right around or during the exact same time they hold their "Admitted Student Days" or "Admitted Student Weekends." That's why "Spring Fly-Ins" are big deals if you get invited to attend them at colleges and universities around the country.

If you have applied for college admission, and then you get an invitation to attend a free Spring Fly-In, but you've not yet been notified about your acceptance, some people see this as very strong interest on the school's part. Such a gesture is said to be a big signal that you will likely get into that college or university. Still, nothing is guaranteed. You won't know for sure until you get your actual acceptance letter.

Richardson, the Tufts official, says the school does some Spring Fly-Ins for admitted students. "We're pretty proactive to reach out to our highest need students," she says. "Especially if they haven't visited our campus, we offer to make their arrangements and to let them stay over night with an undergrad."

Strategy #5: Compare the Pros and Cons of a Group Versus Individual Tour

For those who can't get a freebie from a college, but are determined to do a long distant college visit, here's how to make that trip more affordable.

Start by figuring out if you should go on your own or consider a packaged group tour to visit colleges of your choice.

If you'd have to take a train or airplane, check the prices of rail tickets and airline fares. Call or get online to get hotel rates. Also calculate how much you'd spend in gas if you drove your own car. If you're planning to rent a vehicle, you can get quotes for that too, without making a reservation just yet.

Carefully consider how many days you'd be on the road and do a projection for how much that might cost. If parents will be traveling with a student, which is likely the case for a multi-day road trip, it's also worth noting how much time and money the parent(s) would lose taking time off from work.

Once you have a good sense of your costs, now it's time to weigh the alternative: a group tour where someone else does the driving.

Various college tour companies offer group tours to students and their families. But to give you a sense of pricing and what's involved, consider the following examples.

A company called College Visits, which leads campus tours nationwide, recently charged $1,535 per person for a five-night/six-day Southeast bus tour of nine colleges that originated out of Washington D.C. A six-night/seven-day excursion out of Boston, which toured 10 New England area schools, cost $1,735 per person. Other tours were offered in Southern California and additional parts of the country.

At first glance, those group tour expenses may sound steep. But these packaged tours do include ground transportation, meals, and overnight accommodations. So some people find it more economical — and simply less work — to spend roughly $3,000 to $3,500 for a student and one parent to do a pre-planned, group-led tour, rather than organize everything on their own.

Some schools even offer their own mini-group tours – for a fee. For example, my oldest daughter received what at first appeared to be a Fly-In invitation from Cornell via email.

"You are cordially invited to attend a two-day field trip to visit Cornell University in Ithaca, NY," the message said. "This tour has been arranged with the Undergraduate Admissions Office and is sponsored by the Cornell Club of Northern New Jersey. Sleeping accommodations are in campus residence halls with undergraduate students from the "Red Carpet Society" as your hosts."

Upon further inspection, we saw that this tour was being provided for a cost of $120, in order to cover "bus transportation, plus brunch and dinner on Sunday."

While it wasn't a campus-paid visit, this type of pre-arranged trip demonstrates how some schools are getting more proactive in courting students and directly providing fee-based, guided tours. At a cost of $120, I'm sure that's cheaper than what we (or any Northern New Jersey family) would've shelled out for an overnight hotel stay, plus food and fuel to fill up the car's tank to make the trip to upstate New York.

Whichever method you choose, going it alone or opting for a guided tour, each has its own pros and cons. So it's up to you to decide not only which strategy would be more cost-effective, but also which travel method suits your comfort level and personal preferences.

Strategy #6: Plan Ahead to Save Time, Money and Effort

If you decide to take that good old-fashioned classic college road trip on your own, perhaps the very best thing you can do is to get organized before you hit the road.

Planning ahead will help you optimize your time and avoiding wasting effort while you're traveling. Some forethought and advance planning can also help you economize and do sufficient homework that will lead to big savings.

So use the following guidelines to make your campus visits more productive, hassle-free, and cost-effective.

For starters, try not to pack too much into a road trip. You should be able to visit one or two campuses in a day, but doing more than that will cause unnecessary grief and stress.

Sometimes, students really like a campus and want to explore the surrounding community. So building a little flexibility into your schedule can go a long way.

If you must travel a long distance by car or plane, however, don't simply visit a single campus. Take a swing at multiple campuses to make the trip worth it. Even if the campuses are totally opposite, that can be good for a college-bound student to see. Sometimes students think they may prefer one type of campus, but then it turns out that they're drawn to a completely different type of college or university environment. Also, it would feel like and incredible waste of time, effort and money if you trudged halfway across the country just to see a single school, and wound up hating it.

At each campus, you should plan to spend at least three hours on campus, more if your schedule allows it and you are interested in seeing or doing more.

During a college visit, you will typically have two types of events arranged: information sessions and campus tours.

Admission officers usually lead information sessions, covering topics like campus academics, the admissions process and financial aid. These sessions may include video presentations and typically last 45-minutes to an hour.

After the information session, or even before it, you can also do a campus tour. College students usually lead campus tours, often walking backward as they provide colorful anecdotes, little-known campus lore, and different stories about academics, social activities, and other aspects of life at the institution.

Campus tours can last from one to two hours, though some can run shorter or even longer, depending on the size of the group and the tour guide's personality and schedule.

A tour is sometimes only as interesting as the guide and the campus itself. Some tour guides are great, candidly answering a ton of questions, fielding oddball queries and giving you the low-down on all things good and bad on a campus. Other tour guides sound like walking history books or encyclopedias, spouting off well-memorized facts and dates about the college or university, without giving you a sense of the campus's soul.

That's why it's important to break away from an organized tour, whether it's a good one or a so-so one. By definition, most campus tour guides are very passionate about their schools and they like being something of a cheerleader for the college or university.

But you don't want to only hear about the good things happening on campus. You want to experience some of it for yourself.

So you should take time after the tour to explore the campus on your own for a bit. Introduce yourself to others and talk to current students to get a sense of whether you can envision yourself making the campus home.

Also, pay close attention to your surroundings.

What do the facilities of interest look like? If you're into drama and the performing arts, for example, is the theater or auditorium top-notch —or is it subpar to what you even have at your high school? What about the science labs or libraries?

How extensive and updated are campus resources? Are the buildings nice and new, old and tattered, or somewhere in-between? Old buildings can be great, especially historic, beautiful, or architecturally significant structures that are rich in character and personality. But an old building that's dilapidated or that lacks modern amenities that students need — such as Wi-Fi access in dorms or the library — could be a problem.

If it's important to you, also ask yourself how much diversity there appears to be on campus? Are students mixing freely with one another or are they self-segregating?

And finally, do the students and staff seem friendly toward you? Does anyone smile or say "hello" or does everyone simply look past you? If you ask, are passersby on campus willing to help you with directions or tell you which is the best local restaurant nearby? Or is everyone doing their own thing, and acting like they can't be bothered to give a newbie the time of day?

These are intangibles, and they may be just your impressions. But your opinion counts. So you should make note (mental or written) of your impressions. This is especially important if you're visiting multiple campuses. After a while, they can all start to blend together, and you don't want to accidentally forget highlights (or lowlights) about any particular college or university.

Planning to Lower Travel Costs

Part of your planning efforts should also involve strategizing to maximize savings on transportation and accommodations.

You'll first have to decide, of course, exactly how you'll get to your desired destinations: will it be by your own car, rental car, train, bus or plane?

To save money by car, you might consider carpooling and splitting the cost of gasoline with someone else if other students (and/or parents) are interested in touring similar campuses. If you'll need a rental, don't forget to take your own GPS when you go out of town! That one move can save you $25 to $50 over the course of a multi-day car rental. It's a simple maneuver, but one you could easily forget if you didn't plan ahead.

To save money by bus or train, use student travel discounts and special promotions. For example, Amtrak has a special program for students called Amtrak Campus Visit Discounts. It gives you 20% off train fares.

To save money via air, book tickets early when possible and use frequent flier miles if available. When my daughter and I did a swing of southern campuses, we used frequent flier miles, and it saved us about $1,500 in airfare alone.

To save money on accommodations, determine upfront where you'll stay: at a hotel, on campus facilities or perhaps with a friend or relative.

Don't be ashamed to ask a school if they'll put up a student for the night if you're planning an out-of-town campus visit. Many schools will, though admittedly accommodations for parents may not be available, so a hotel room will still be necessary. But you never know until you ask.

If you have family in the area, it certainly could be a money-saver if you can crash there for a few days while you're in town.

When you must book a hotel, consider using websites like Priceline. com for rock-bottom pricing on hotel stays. Also, take advantage of discounted hotel rates if you have memberships with AAA or AARP. Those memberships typically save you 10% to 15% or so off your hotel bill.

Strategy #7: Get Reimbursements, Tuition Credit and Other Perks

The final thing you should do is seek ways to make the trip pay off financially.

College Secret:

Lots of institutions will give you travel reimbursements for visiting their campuses. You just have to ask for them, and know how to qualify for these incentives.

Many students and their families don't realize that there are lots of ways to receive economic benefits from a campus visit. Here are some ideas for receiving financial offsets and other economic perks you deserve when you go on campus tours.

How to Ask for Campus Travel Reimbursements

Short of nabbing one of those coveted "Fly-In" deals, one of the next best things you can get is travel reimbursement from a college or university.

Scores of colleges offer travel reimbursements, because they realize that it's financially costly for far-away students to visit in person.

Here is a small sampling of the numerous and varied travel reimbursements offered by post-secondary schools nationwide:

- Bryant University has a Fly-In program, and reimburses students for up to $300.
- Colorado Christian University has a $300 Airfare Reimbursement Program.
- Dakota Wesleyan University has a travel reimbursement of up to $500 for visits.
- Eastern Nazarene College has a travel reimbursement program of $300 to $500.
- Southern Virginia University has a $250 reimbursement for campus visits.
- The College of Idaho has a Fly-In Reimbursement of half a plane ticket, up to $150
- UC Berkeley's Integrative Biology Department offers a $300 to $600 travel reimbursement.
- University of Evansville has a Fly-In program, reimbursing students up to $400.

As you can see, just asking for a travel reimbursement can shave several hundreds of dollars off campus touring expenses.

Needless to say, every campus has its own specific rules and guidelines about how people qualify for a travel reimbursement. Some will give it to any student who travels a certain distance, such as 200 miles or more.

Other schools will give you a travel reimbursement or travel credit — but only after you've applied, been accepted, and then registered as a student. That's the case at Drexel University in Philadelphia. Prospective freshmen and transfer students who live at least 150 miles away from Drexel and still pay a visit to campus are eligible to recoup up to $500 of their travel costs, should they later be accepted and choose to attend the school. Likewise, Central College has a travel reimbursement up to $250, but only after admission.

You'll only know by doing a bit of homework, and checking out a school's website for this information. Alternatively, you can simply call the admissions office, explain that you will be visiting from a faraway location, and ask whether or not travel assistance is available.

Earn Tuition Credit for Your Campus Visit

Another financial payout you can receive simply for making a campus visit is tuition credit. Again, numerous colleges provide this benefit for those savvy enough to ask.

Here's a brief look at some schools that provide a credit toward your tuition if you visit the campus and later enroll.

- Loyola University in New Orleans offers a $1,000 tuition credit for all official campus visits
- National University of Health Sciences offers a $250 to $500 tuition credit
- Stevenson University has a $250 tuition credit for campus visits

Colleges like Loyola, Stevenson and others are offering these tuition credits as a way to incentivize students to make in-person, pre-college visits.

So remember to always document your expenses, keep your travel receipts, and sign in for group tours or information sessions so that colleges and universities have a record of your campus visit. That's a good practice for other reasons, too. Remember: admission officers view contact initiated by students (including campus visits) as one indication of demonstrated interest.

Get Free or Discounted Meals, Housing and Other Perks

When you participate in an information session or campus tour, it's very common for school officials to give you meal tickets for free or discounted meals in a student dining hall. Alternatively, some colleges will give you booklets with coupons or reduced fare options for nearby restaurants.

Take advantage of these free and low-cost deals as a way to reduce your meal expenses while you're on the road.

Know too that some schools go beyond meal freebies. So it never hurts to ask what financial rebates, discounts or incentives schools provide for campus visits.

Walla Walla University, for instance, has a generous reimbursement policy for those visiting, including airfare reimbursement up to $250, free housing and meals.

Similarly, Calvin College offers a $200 reimbursement, housing and free meals for students of color who visit.

Students who visit Cedar Crest College in Allentown, PA and later get admitted receive a one-time $500 scholarship.

"Cedar Crest College understands the need for college to be a good 'fit,'" says Ann Sywensky, an assistant in the school's admissions office. "We believe that a campus visit is an important part of determining 'fit.'"

So Cedar Crest College has partnered with www.RAISE.me to provide incentives for campus visits, those taking honors or AP courses, performing community service and other important high school achievements. Students create a profile at RAISE and are given merit aid developed by Cedar Crest that rewards positive high school behaviors.

Elsewhere, at least for one school, a campus visit can also pay off by later reducing another big expense you'll face down the road: college textbooks. At the University of Dayton, if you visit the Ohio campus, complete the FAFSA and get accepted, the school will provide you with four years' worth of textbooks for free.

Tips About Visits for Recruited Athletes

There is one other form of free visit that I've not yet mentioned. It concerns visits by recruited athletes.

If you play an individual or team sport and you are being actively recruited, some college coaches may offer you an all-expense-paid trip to go visit their campuses. Obviously, they're doing this to entice you to join their sports program.

But realize that there are two types of visits for athletes: unofficial and official. An *unofficial* visit is one you make on your own to a college or university. Maybe a coach has called you and expressed interest, or perhaps he or she had said something along the lines of "It would be nice if you could visit." Under such circumstances, they want to learn more about you, but you're really not being *actively* recruited. At this point, you're simply one of many, many students they have on their radar.

On the other hand, an official visit is a two-day trip to a college or university that's fully paid for by the school. This is a much stronger sign of interest from a campus, since a college or university that's willing to invest money to get you to their school is clearly very seriously considering where you might fit in at that particular institution. As an athlete, you are generally only allowed a total of five official visits.

So if you should you get such an offer, do take advantage of it. But if you're highly sought after — and some recruited athletes are — it's wise to be selective in your visits. Don't just take the first five offers that come along, because you wouldn't be able to take free campus trips to other, more attractive schools you may want to attend.

When you go on an official visit, don't simply check out the athletics program at a college or university. Even for the brief period that you're there, try to get to know all aspects of the college: connect with other students (including non-athletes), talk to a professor or two, and see if you can envision yourself at that particular school.

Know also that your parents can go with you on official visits. They may be able to provide some valuable perspective — and help you keep your head on straight — when it seems that everyone is wooing you and acting as if they can give you the world on a silver platter.

If an Ivy League school invites you for an official campus visit, you're in even more rare company. Ivy League colleges are allowed to host just 70 official visits. However, they only get to keep 35 players.

By using the seven strategies outlined in this chapter, you can make the process of conducting campus tours and visits far more manageable and productive, and less taxing on your wallet as well.

COLLEGE APPLICATIONS

I was once on College Confidential's message boards when I came across a post from a teenager lamenting that her parents didn't have the money to give her the $50 she needed for a college application.

It broke my heart to realize that some families are really so cash-strapped that they can't even afford college application fees, let alone college tuition.

But going to college can often be the best shot that many poor kids have for opportunity and a better chance in life.

So when I think about how many students must be in that teen girl's same position, it's really distressing — and it should bother all of us.

No matter what your family income, college applications aren't cheap — especially if you're filling out numerous applications, as most students do during college application season.

According to a recent survey from U.S. News, the average application fee that 1,229 ranked institutions provided was $38.79, the highest it's been in six years. For the top 28 schools with the priciest applications, the average application fee was $77 — twice the national average. Most competitive schools charge students $50 and above to submit an application.

Accountant Ed Fulbright remembers when his daughter — who is now a student at the University of North Carolina at Chapel Hill — was applying to multiple schools.

"She's fiercely independent, and she filled out all her applications herself," he recalls, adding with a laugh: "The only time we ever saw them was to give her the credit card to pay the application fees."

All joking aside, let's say you apply to 10 schools (not uncommon these days) and the average cost of each application is $50. Bam! There goes $500, yet another hit to the family budget as you deal with ever-rising college costs.

That money is spent just to give you a *shot* at getting into college. Since the admission process is fraught with uncertainty — thanks to a host of school variables and a slew of subjective factors — your application to any one particular college is rarely a sure bet. In most cases, no one can say with 100% confidence that you'll get accepted into any specific four-year school. Nevertheless, college application fees are almost universally non-refundable fees. What's more, even though you might submit 10 applications, in reality you can only attend one school at a time.

Using Application Waivers To Save Hundreds of Dollars

For all these reasons, this chapter is devoted to explaining eight ways students can get fee waivers for college applications. A fee waiver will let you apply at no cost to the college of your choice, keeping money in your bank account and lowering your pre-college expenses.

The eight college application fee waiver strategies are:

1. Get a fee waiver based on economic need
2. Get a fee waiver for being a great student
3. Get a fee waiver for visiting a campus or going to a college fair
4. Get a fee waiver for applying to or attending a "Fly-In" program
5. Get a fee waiver for special circumstances
6. Get a fee waiver for service activities
7. Get a fee waiver for applying early
8. Get a fee waiver for being a child of a veteran or a college employee

Let's look at each one of these strategies and how they can help you to save hundreds of dollars in college application costs.

After we deal with the financial aspects of college applications, we'll address a related topic that I know is of great interest to students and parents alike: your statistical chances of having a winning application that gets you accepted into the schools of your choice.

Get a Fee Waiver Based on Economic Need

If you need a waiver to submit a college application, you can get one from one of three sources: the NACAC, the College Board (which administers the SAT), and the college or university where you want to apply.

NACAC and SAT application waivers are only available for U.S. citizens. The same is true for most institutional waivers, though international students should check with their target schools to confirm their individual rules and policies.

Regardless of which entity provides the fee waiver — the NACAC, the College Board or a specific post-secondary school — the most common way to get a waiver for a college application is to qualify for one based on economic need.

You can use a number of methods to prove that you have a genuine economic need for an application fee waiver. One such way that colleges determine economic need is simply based on your household income. Remember Chapter 2, which discussed getting fee waivers for standardized college entrance exams? Well, the same income guidelines apply for college applications.

In general, you may qualify for an application fee waiver if your annual household income is about $45,000 or so, assuming a family of four. However, qualifying income levels can be more or less than that figure, depending on the number of people in your household. Other income-related qualifications will get you waivers too — such as qualifying for free or reduced lunch.

You can obtain a NACAC fee waiver, called a "Request for Waiver of College Application Fee" form, from your high school counselor. Likewise, if you were eligible for a fee waiver for the SAT or SAT Subject Tests, you can ask your high school counselor to give you up to four fee waivers for your college applications.

You simply fill out the top portion of either form (the NACAC waiver or the SAT fee waiver), have a high school counselor or other third party sign it, then turn in the form along with your college application. This way, you need not send in an application fee.

The NACAC form outlines a host of circumstances that make students economically qualified to get waivers for college application fees. Among those circumstances:

- You are eligible to receive an SAT or ACT fee waiver
- You are enrolled in or eligible to participate in the free or reduced lunch program at school
- Your family income falls within the income Eligibility Guidelines set by the USDA Food and Nutrition Service
- You are enrolled in a federal, state or local program that aids low-income students (i.e. TRIO programs, like Upward Bound)
- Your family receives public assistance (such as food stamps — nationwide about 47 million Americans, roughly 15% of all citizens, receive food stamps)
- You live in federally subsidized public housing, a foster home, or are homeless
- You are a ward of the state or an orphan
- You face any other challenges that would make paying college application fees a financial hardship

Note two specific points about the first circumstance described, and the last scenario.

For the first situation, realize that you may have taken the SAT or ACT but not actually *received* a waiver for test fees. That doesn't mean you can't get a College Board/SAT college application fee waiver. Colleges only require that you be *eligible* for an SAT waiver — not that you actually *use* a waiver.

For the last scenario, be aware that a high school principal, school counselor, financial aid officer, or community leader must not only sign the form, but must also briefly explain your individual extenuating circumstances.

Also, in *all* the circumstances listed above, a signature from a third party is mandatory to use a fee waiver from NACAC.

If your school doesn't have NACAC waiver forms, you can obtain a fee waiver form from the NACAC website.

The process for using a fee waiver is pretty easy if you are filling out college applications online. Once you get to the "Payment" section, which comes right *before* you submit your application, just indicate that you are using a waiver. That will allow your web-based college application to be accepted and processed.

Most two- and four-year colleges (about 80% of them) do honor fee waivers granted by both the College Board and NACAC. You can find an online list of schools that accept SAT application fee waivers at the SAT Fee Waiver Directory of Colleges. The NACAC does not maintain a directory of colleges that accept its waiver request form.

Another thing to keep in mind for the future is that students going on to graduate school, or those seeking degrees in specialty areas, such as law school, business school or medical school, can also get fee waivers for your graduate school applications. If you received a fee waiver to take an exam, you typically also qualify for fee waivers for graduate school applications.

Assume you later want to go to law school at the University of Virginia. If you received a waiver for the LSAT or LSDAS fees from the Law School Admission Council, you will automatically qualify for an application fee waiver from the University of Virginia when you apply electronically through LSAC.

As a final tip regarding fee waivers, some of you may be wondering how many of these you can use.

The NACAC recommends that you use their waiver request form at a maximum of four colleges. Such a recommendation or suggestion is obviously not an ironclad prohibition against utilizing the waiver for more than four college applications. Therefore, if you really need to apply to five schools using NACAC waivers, you can certainly do so. Just exercise this option very judiciously. You don't want to abuse these fee waivers nor should you ever misrepresent your economic circumstances. Besides, accepting a fee waiver is always at the final discretion of the college or university anyway.

A better strategy if you are applying to more than four schools is to use *both* the NACAC fee waiver request form *and* the College Board's SAT fee waivers.

These waivers are mutually exclusive and totally independent of one another. So you can use, say, the NACAC fee waiver form at four schools, then use the SAT Fee waiver at four different institutions, covering a total of eight college applications. This should cover the vast majority of students who require waivers for college.

College Secret:

Despite conventional wisdom, if you qualify for application fee waivers, you can use those waivers to apply to 8 (or more) college campuses at no cost.

Get a Fee Waiver for Being a Great Student

Being a student who gets terrific grades and tests extremely well provides a lot of benefits. There's the self-satisfaction you get in knowing you did your best and achieved at the highest levels. There's the hug or pat on the back you get from proud parents. You might also earn special recognition, such as landing a spot on the honor roll at school, being inducted into the National Honor Society, or being named a National Merit Scholarship semifinalist or finalist.

If you're an academic standout, that status can also offer advantages when it comes to college admissions. Stellar grades — say, at the top 10% of your class — will usually put your college application in or near the top of the pile when you're applying to most colleges. Great test scores and academic honors get noticed too, especially if they're based on nationwide testing.

Fortunately, there's one other benefit to being a scholarly student. You may find that some schools will reward you by waiving their application fees just to encourage you to apply.

For example, the University of Maryland grants fee waivers for National Merit, National Achievement, or National Hispanic finalists or semi-finalists and Maryland Distinguished Scholar finalists, semi-finalists, and honorable mention recipients.

Other campuses award application fee waivers to students with a certain minimum grade point average, such as a 3.5 GPA or higher or even a 3.0 GPA or better.

If you are an especially high-achieving student, peruse college websites or call the schools you're interested in and ask whether fee waivers are available for select scholars.

Get a Fee Waiver for Visiting a Campus or Going to a College Fair

Simply going to visit a campus or attending a college fair may be enough to get you a fee waiver. Often, college recruiters will pass out special forms or codes you can use while you're online applying to the school in order to take advantage of the fee waiver.

So anytime you take a campus tour or participate in a college fair, don't simply skip over the materials on the desks. See whether any of them are fee waivers for applicants.

Get a Fee Waiver for Applying to or Attending a "Fly-In" Program

Certain Fly-In programs offer application fee waivers to students who attend early recruitment programs. One example is the Future Achievers of Science and Technology, or FAST Programs, at Harvey Mudd College. Not only are FAST programs absolutely free for selected seniors and juniors, those program participants also receive a fee waiver so they don't have to pay the school's usual $70 fee charged for freshman applications.

Even if you don't get into a Fly-In program, simply *applying* to attend one of these free campus visits could make you eligible for a college application fee waiver. That's the case with Amherst, which gives a fee waiver for its $60 application to students selected to attend the school's Diversity Open House, as well as students who apply to the Fly-In Program but who are not invited. The fee waiver is intended to encourage that latter group of students to still consider Amherst and apply to the school.

Get a Fee Waiver for Special Circumstances

If you or a key family member has recently experienced a great financial hardship or a major change in household or economic circumstances, many schools will waive their application fees, as long as you explain and document those circumstances.

Fee waivers can be obtained for issues such as: recent job loss, a death in the family (of a main breadwinner), enormous medical bills, homelessness, personal tragedy, economic complications stemming from natural calamities or other disasters, and more. These fee waiver requests are evaluated and granted on a case-by-case basis. Schools also require that a third party, such as a guidance counselor, teacher, school official with knowledge of the student's extenuating circumstances sign the NACAC form requesting the application fee waiver.

You should also be aware of what won't cut it in terms of getting you a fee waiver. On its website, Rice University states: "Financial stress created by application fees to other institutions is not considered a valid reason to grant a fee waiver." Other colleges echo this sentiment. So if you make an appeal for a waiver based on special circumstances, don't say it's because you're applying to so many other colleges! That won't generate a lot of sympathy.

Get a Fee Waiver for Service Activities

You also may be eligible for a waived application fee if you've performed any number of service activities and are an alumnus of different service-based groups. For instance, those who have been in Teach for America, the Peace Corps, Americorps/VISTA, CityYear, or in various fellowships, such as a Truman Public Service Fellowship, can have their college application fees waived.

As a practical matter, service-based fee waivers will typically be utilized by older individuals applying to college, as opposed to teen students coming straight out of high school. But if you fit the profile and you qualify, do seek your fee waiver as part of an overall strategy to control your pre-college expenses.

To get this kind of fee waiver, contact the schools you're interested in directly. You won't be able to use a fee waiver from NACAC.

Non-traditional students are not eligible to use NACAC's fee waiver form. This applies to gap year students, transfer students, as well as those opting to defer applying to college instead of immediately attending a college or university right after high school graduation.

Get a Fee Waiver for Applying Early

In the college application process, you can apply for admission during various times. The college application season has a variety of distinct cycles, the most common of which are known as Regular Decision, Early Decision and Early Action.

Regular Decision simply means that you submit your application during the normal application cycle. This usually occurs in December or January for most schools.

Applying Early Decision is done when you have strong interest in one specific school and you know with certainty that you want to attend that school above all others. So when you apply Early Decision, you are essentially making a binding commitment that if a school accepts you (assuming you can afford that institution), you'll withdraw your other college applications and go to the school that has granted you admission via Early Decision. Early Decision applications are usually due around November.

Early Action is a similar application process where a student opts to apply early to a school, typically around November or December, but isn't *bound* to go to that school if accepted.

There is also a fourth way to categorize the timing of college applications, under an admissions method known as rolling admissions. Colleges and universities that have rolling admissions accept college applications on an ongoing or "rolling" basis until classes are full.

The key thing to know about all this, from a financial standpoint, is that some schools look favorably upon early applicants. Interest in early applicants is so high that various schools will even waive their application fees.

For instance, at Drew University in Madison, New Jersey, which normally has a $50 application fee, the application fees of all Early Decision applicants are automatically waived. At Whitman College in Walla Walla, Washington, the school's Regular Decision deadline is January 15. But Regular Decision applicants to the college get an automatic waiver of the school's $50 application fee, provided students submit their applications early, by December 1.

Upon entering her senior year, my daughter received many, many invitations to apply early from colleges nationwide. Many campuses sent special "VIP" "Fast-Track" or "Priority Applications" that waived their application fees. Obviously, if you get such applications, either in the mail or online, from any of your target schools, then you should use those applications in order to save money.

College Secret:

> If you're applying early to a college, ask for a fee waiver. Even if a school doesn't officially grant waivers to early applicants, it may still give you one upon request.

Get a Fee Waiver for Being a Child of a Veteran or a College Employee

Some students can qualify for fee waivers on the basis of their parents' affiliation or job. For example, certain colleges grant application waivers to veterans, and to children of veterans as well.

Additionally, having a parent who already works at a college or university can be a bonus when it comes to college applications. A number of post-secondary schools give the offspring of faculty, staff, and administrative personnel a break on college application fees. Case in point: Within the California State University system, those 23 campuses waive their customary application fees for children of full-time and permanent part-time university employees.

Reduce College Application Fees by Applying Online

If you are unable to use the eight strategies described above to get full waivers of your application fees, you may at least be able to cut the fees at some schools.

Certain colleges have lower application fees when you apply online, as opposed to submitting a paper application.

For example, if you mail a paper-based application to George Mason University, that document will cost you a hefty $100 — the priciest application in the nation. But George Mason officials drop the application cost by 40% to $60 for those applying online.

Some schools take it one step further, eliminating application fees altogether if students use the web. Drexel University's paper application fee is $75. However, it's completely free for online applicants.

Cut Costs by Using an Application Fee Deferment

You don't want a lack of money to prohibit you from applying to a college or university. So it's good news (and it may come as a surprise to you) that some schools will let you defer paying an application fee until you enroll.

Consider the normal application fee of $40 that is required at Iowa's Regent Universities (Iowa State, University of Iowa and University of Northern Iowa). If paying the $40 fee would be an economic hardship, applicants can simply turn in their applications on time, and then get charged the application fee as part of their college bill when they enroll in August.

For this to happen, a student must submit a brief letter requesting the fee deferment and explaining that paying the fee upfront would be a financial hardship. Anyone can write the letter, including the student, a relative, a school counselor, or someone from an outside group, such as a TRiO advisor.

If you did apply to each of those Iowa schools, using a deferment option would save you $80 because you'd later only have to pay the application fee at one of the three state schools — the one where you ultimately enrolled.

Lack of Info About Waivers Hurts High School Students

With such an abundance of ways to get fee wavers and reduced fees for college applications, it's a shame that more eligible students don't take advantage of these cost savers.

I'm convinced that students pay needlessly for college-related items or don't get the educational support and resources they need and deserve because they simply don't know about these things. Moreover, their parents and peers may not know, and neither do some counselors.

Even more disturbing, many students don't have a school counselor at all.

According to a 2014 report from the U.S. Department of Education, nationwide one in five schools lack a school counselor. And in some states, like Florida and Minnesota, more than 40% of students don't have a counselor.

When counselors are present in high schools, they are often overwhelmed.

In public schools, the student-to-counselor ratio is now running at a staggering 421-to-1. Yes, you read that correctly: on average in the U.S. there is just 1 high school counselor for every 421 students. (Ratios at private high schools are much lower).

Technological innovations can sometimes help. For example, a new website called Admittedly, serves as a sort of personal online counselor. Fonded in 2013 by former private college admissions counselor Jessica Brondo, Admittedly helps students find schools that would be a good match for them based on the applicant's academic background, personal interests and other factors.

Recently the website launched a feature called Major Matcher to help students select college majors suitable to their interests. It also debuted the College Visit planner, Application Manager, and Essay Advisor in 2014, with additional modules focused on Financial Aid & Scholarships, Test Prep, as well as the Improve My Chances module, to launch in 2015.

Nonetheless, the lack of information and adequate counselor support leads students of all backgrounds — both low-income and wealthy — to turn to outside help with college applications.

College applications are crucial, so getting assistance with these forms can be a smart move. But be wary of paying exorbitant costs for such help or doling out money to someone who will simply fill out elements of your application that you can on your own.

There is a cottage industry of current and former admissions officers, financial aid counselors, and other educational consultants who specialize in advising students on their college applications. Some of these experts are better than others. And needless to say, some have low and moderately priced services, while others have exorbitant fees.

At the high end of the market, families who want their kids to get college application help from places like ApplicationBootcamp.com pay $14,000 for a four-day session.

Over this four-day period, students work one-on-one with the company's founders and a team of college specialists in Cambridge, Massachusetts. By the end of the Boot Camp, students have completed their Common Applications; prepared college essays; created an activity sheet summarizing their high school awards, activities and achievement; and received customized advice to increase their odds of college admission.

For those who can't swing the $14,000 price tag, a la carte services are also available. For instance, getting five hours of one-on-one phone help with a college essay from ApplicationBootcamp.com costs $2,500.

Clearly, these services are for well-heeled families (or those simply willing to go into debt).

But you can certainly find far, far more affordable help with college applications if you truly need it.

However, most students don't pay for help with their college applications at all. They simply tackle the forms on their own, or get free input from teachers, guidance counselors, and older siblings in college, or other adults and mentors experienced in the college application process.

In the 2013-2014 school year, a total of 754,545 students filled out the Common Application.

Of all students filling out the Common App, 71% had at least one parent with a Bachelor's Degree, and 29% were first-generation college students.

The Common App Makes It Tougher To Get In

Speaking of the Common App, it's worth knowing a little bit of history about this important tool — and how this application affects your chances of gaining college admission.

The Common Application began as a paper document in 1975, and back then only 15 colleges accepted the form.

Students had to painstakingly photocopy their applications and then mail them to the colleges of their choice, along with separate application fees to each institution. Because of the cumbersome, time-consuming nature of that process, only 3.2% of students applied to seven or more colleges in 1975, according to surveys of college freshmen conducted nationwide by UCLA.

In 1998, the online Common App was created, making it far easier to submit numerous applications to colleges.

For the 2014-2015 school year, 548 colleges and universities accepted the Common Application. During the preceding school term, college-bound students submitted 3.3 million applications via the Common App, which worked out to an average of 4.4 applications per student.

More than 27% of students applied to at least seven colleges or universities.

The next-generation Common Application Online, dubbed CA4, launched on August 1, 2013, and was billed as "a revolutionary new platform" to "improve the online experience." Upgrades to the Common App include: "smart questions," onscreen support, progress checks, and streamlined CEEB/School Search methods.

But during the 2013-2014 school year, users of CA4 experienced a lot of technical problems and glitches. Those issues have now been fixed — and thankfully so, since CA4 is an online-only application. The application is no longer available in paper form or as a downloadable document for mailing.

Because of these and other changes, a New York Times article forecast that the number of applications filed through the Common Application portal by the end of this decade could exceed 10 million — and the number of schools accepting it could grow to 1,000 or more.

If that prediction proves even remotely accurate, then the technological ease of simultaneously applying to multiple schools will continue to drive record numbers of applications at colleges nationwide — fueling another current trend in the world of college: hyper-selectivity.

Selectivity is simply a measure of how many applicants were accepted by a given school versus the number of students who applied. To describe a college's selectivity, we usually use a percentage figure. So if 10,000 applicants applied to a school and 2,000 were accepted, you could say the campus was a highly selective school that admitted just 20% of those who applied.

Colleges that accept less than half of all applicants are considered to be selective. The lower the acceptance rate, the more selective the institution is deemed. These schools typically get far more applications than their less selective peers.

Are the Odds *Really* Stacked Against You?

UCLA broke the record for every college in the country when it received an unprecedented 86,521 applications from would-be freshman hoping to attend the school starting in the fall of 2014. With so many students vying for limited spots, is it any wonder that only 18.2% of students were given the chance to join the Bruin family?

Meanwhile, Ivy League schools were even more selective. Admission rates for all of these campuses were in the single digits or low double-digits for students applying to become freshmen in the fall for the Class of 2018.

For example, a look at those admission decisions reveals that:

- Harvard accepted only 5.9% of its 34,295 applicants;
- Yale took a scant 6.3% of its 30,932 applicants;
- Columbia admitted just 6.9% of its 32,967 applicants;
- Princeton said yes to only 7.3% of its 26,641 applicants;
- Brown accepted 8.6% of its 30,432 applicants;
- Penn granted entry to a mere 10% of its 35,868 applicants
- Dartmouth granted entry to a 11.5% of its 19,296 applicants
- Cornell offered spots to 14% of 43,041 applicants

What this means is that for most Ivy League schools, 90% or more of the students who applied to those campuses were *rejected* — despite most of them being outstanding scholars on paper.

The same thing happened at other ultra selective schools such as Stanford and MIT. Stanford had the lowest acceptance rate in the country, giving the thumbs up to a slim 5% of the 42,167 students that applied for the Class of 2018. MIT accepted only 8% of its 18,357 applicants.

Students need to know that great grades and terrific test scores are no longer the passport for entry into America's top colleges. In truth, that's been the case for years. But the bar for entry is even higher now because so many well-qualified students are applying to multiple schools.

And this phenomena isn't limited to Ivy League schools and top private institutions like Stanford and MIT. Many excellent public and state schools are also becoming more selective.

But are the odds truly stacked against college-bound students?

The answer is a resounding "no" — despite what you might read, see or hear in the media.

The Truth About College Admission and Acceptance Rates

Here's the truth about college admission: It's true that certain schools are getting more selective. But it's also the case that Ivy League statistics and the acceptance rates at other elite private and public schools are not even remotely indicative of overall college acceptance rates.

The vast majority of U.S. colleges and universities welcome an extremely high percentage of students with open arms. In fact, nationwide, the average college accepts 67% of all applicants, figures from NACAC's latest State of College Admission report show.

It's also true that most students are not — I repeat, are <u>not</u> — crying the blues about being shut out of their dream schools. In fact, three out of four students (76%) get accepted into their *first-choice school*, according to The American Freshman: National Norms, an annual survey conducted by UCLA's Higher Education Research Institute.

Finally, it's important to note that more than 75% of all four-year colleges and universities in the U.S. accept more than half of their applicants. When you include community colleges, the numbers are even more encouraging. Community colleges accept 100% of students who apply.

College Secret:

76% of high-school applicants get accepted into their first-choice colleges. So don't believe misleading reports suggesting that colleges are rejecting students en masse.

Looking at higher education from this broader perspective, you can easily see that there is truly a college for anyone who wants to attend.

So what's going on here with all the hype about razor-thin college admission rates? And why does it seem that we always hear, from friends and the media, about so many outstanding students — those with near-perfect test scores and stellar grades — getting their college hopes dashed by their top choice schools?

It's because for those students, their top choice schools were almost invariably among the single-most selective campuses in the nation.

When students with 4.0 GPAs reportedly get rejected from every single college to which they've applied, one of the issues is that they focused all their efforts on the top 30 or so schools in the United States. Some even applied only to campuses ranked in the *top 10* of all national universities or liberal arts colleges.

That kind of focus on brand-name institutions is insane.

"What it does to high school students is a shame," says college expert Lucie Lapovsky. She adds: "A lot of it is bragging rights for the parents. In certain neighborhoods, it's manic. Everyone is crazy about where their kids are going to college."

As a result, some youth — often egged on by overzealous parents — have made the unfortunate and completely avoidable mistake of putting all of their eggs in one basket: the elite school basket, which is comprised of only the top 1% to 4% of all U.S. colleges.

Instead of having a more reasonable admission strategy — applying to a couple "reach" schools, several "target" schools and a few "safety" schools — they applied mostly (or in some cases, exclusively) to schools with acceptance rates below 20%.

What are these campuses? In addition to those previously mentioned, for the class of 2018, Olin accepted only 10.2% of applicants — Duke 10.7%, Vanderbilt 11%, Pomona 12.2%, Amherst College 12.8%, Northwestern 12.9%, Harvey Mudd 13.2%, Bowdoin 14.9%, Johns Hopkins 15%, Middlebury 17.4%, and USC 17.8%.

Sadly, some students and parents feel that the only schools "worth" attending are brand-name institutions. And since it's very difficult to remove this bumper sticker mentality, the nation's most selective colleges always receive a disproportionate number of applications compared to the limited number of spots they have available for first-year students.

One consequence of this phenomenon is that the admit rates at very prestigious national universities and top liberal arts colleges are far lower than at other schools.

But please, don't get discouraged or misled into thinking that increased selectivity among a tiny portion of colleges and universities is reflective of the big picture within higher education.

Nothing could be further from the truth.

If you talk to any good college advisor, those experts try to get students to expand their college horizons and consider a variety of institutions that could be a great fit.

"Students need to go where they feel comfortable," Lapovsky says, "and when students are in the top 10% of their class, they do really well at almost any school they attend."

College expert Lynn O'Shaughnessy, the author of *The College Solution* and a financial workbook called *Shrinking the Cost of College*, agrees.

"Part of this fixation on just three or four dozen schools is that parents and students don't know about a whole lot of great schools out there that just aren't on people's radar," says O'Shaughnessy, who also runs a helpful blog, TheCollegeSolution.com.

"Most people have no idea that there are more than 2,200 four-year schools in America. So it's just a lack of knowledge," she says. "But if you only focus on the most well-known schools, you're going to be disappointed because those are the ones that the most ambitious, and often most affluent, students want to go to. So students simply need to cast a wider net and to look at more schools than they might initially consider."

Also realize that your future happiness doesn't depend on which college you attend, but rather what you do with the opportunities you get while in college.

A recent Gallup poll, conducted with Purdue University, found that students who were happier in their work and personal lives after college graduation were those individuals who had meaningful, memorable experiences while they were in school.

Gallup researchers found that "the type of schools these college graduates attended — public or private, small or large, very selective or less selective — hardly matters at all to their workplace engagement and current well-being."

Instead, the study found that *"support and experiences in college had more of a relationship to long-term outcomes for these college graduates. For example, if graduates recalled having a professor who cared about them as a person, made them excited about learning, and encouraged them to pursue their dreams, their odds of being engaged at work more than doubled, as did their odds of thriving in all aspects of their well-being. And if graduates had an internship or job in college where they were able to apply what they were learning in the classroom, were actively involved in extracurricular activities and organizations, and worked on projects that took a semester or more to complete, their odds of being engaged at work doubled as well."*

College Secret:

Studies show that where you go to college doesn't determine your happiness post-graduation. It's all about *what you do* on *any* given campus.

Unfortunately, far too few students had the type of enriching college experiences that carried with them after graduation. Only 14% of graduates said they "strongly agree" that they were supported by professors who cared, who made them excited about learning, and who encouraged their dreams. Additionally, just 6% of graduates strongly agree they had an internship or job that allowed them to apply what they were learning, worked on a long-term project, and were actively involved in extra-curricular activities. So in picking a school, instead of chasing prestige, focus on four things: academic and personal fit, campus opportunities and affordability. That's the best strategy to ensure your happiness in college and life after college.

CHAPTER 9

ᏚHE ᏚEST ᏚAYS TO ᏚAVE FOR ᏚOLLEGE

For those of you who are parents, it's understandable that you want to help your child avoid the plague of student loan debt, but there's a right way to go about doing it — and a wrong way.

The wrong way is to completely sacrifice your financial future, forgoing retirement savings and just "hoping for the best" when you're in your golden years. The right way is to approach college with some smart financial planning. Use the following tips to reduce the student loan burden that you and your kid will face later in life.

Save for College as Early as Possible

You already know that college is expensive right now, but what about the future? Well, the annual price tag for higher education is estimated to swell by at least 5% or more each year, pushing costs upward at public and private universities as well. Unfortunately, about one-third of parents who plan to help pay for college haven't started saving yet. Start socking away as much as you can now to decrease the need for loans in the future.

"The Number 1 financial mistake people make in planning for college is not starting to save soon enough," says Suzanna De Baca, vice president of wealth strategies at Ameriprise Financial. "Many folks know that college is looming on the horizon. But in your 20s or 30s, there are many competing priorities and those with young children think that college is so far down the road."

"The second biggest mistake," DeBaca adds, "is underestimating the true total cost of college."

O'Shaughnessy, the college expert, is living proof of the power of saving early. She and her husband finished paying for their two children's college education in 2014 and they did it the old fashioned way — without any loans at all.

"Our strategy was pretty unsexy," O'Shaughnessy says, "just starting early, saving as much as possible, and trying to pick quality schools."

Open a 529 Plan

A 529 college savings plan is the best thing going when it comes to saving for your child's college education. Available in every state in the country, a 529 plan is portable and can be used at any qualifying institution of higher learning in America. It's a great way to sock away tens of thousands of dollars annually for higher educational expenses because money in a 529 plan grows tax free if it's used for college costs.

Many states even give you a tax deduction for contributing to a 529. Best of all: these plans are maintained in the parent's (or the donor's) name, so they don't reduce a child's chances for receiving financial aid. For more info on 529 plans, visit http://www.savingforcollege.com, which is run by Joe Hurley, the top 529 guru in the U.S. (Read on at the end of these tips for more detailed info on 529 plans).

Plan for Some Aid – But Be Realistic

If you're a parent, unless you can truly afford it without changing your whole lifestyle, strike a balance between trying to fund your kids' college account, and planning to get some need-based aid. There's no rule that says you have to foot your son or daughter's entire college tuition bills, plus pay for all his or her living expenses and other needs.

Apply for aid, but don't over-estimate how much your child will get from any given school or outside source of funding. Although many parents think their kids will get a "full ride" to cover all college costs, the reality is that only 0.3% of students, or about 20,000 students annually do, according to research from college financing expert Mark Kantrowitz, Publisher of Edvisors.com. Also, just 7% or so of college students win private college scholarships, with awards averaging in the $2,500 range, according to Kantrowitz, who is also the author of Secrets to Winning a Scholarship.

College Secret:

Less than 1% of all college and university students in America get a "full ride," with all expenses paid. So be realistic in your scholarship and aid expectations.

Your child's financial aid package will be based on your income and assets, the cost of the school, the school's own financial aid policies, and whether you have other children in college.

Take your entire situation into account when you're thinking about aid. Do you have more kids or other family members who will need money for school or other reasons? Also be mindful of your own income picture — not to mention rising healthcare costs, current bills, and the need to save for your own retirement.

Use Smart Tools to Forecast Financial Aid

If you're heading to college or grad school, you can get a sense of how much financial aid you're likely to qualify for by using the FAFSA4caster.

FAFSA stands for Free Application for Federal Student Aid. Filling out the FAFSA early or on time is crucial to maximizing your financial aid and lowering your out-of-pocket costs. No matter your family's income, this is the form to fill out. Based on the information you provide FAFSA, you may receive financial aid in the form of government-supported student loans, or grants (that you won't need to pay back!). If you receive a grant to attend an institution, you can lower your tuition expenses without adding to your student debt. Applying for financial aid also makes you eligible for college work-study programs, which can further cut your need for loans.

It's wise to complete the FAFSA as early as possible, preferably in January each year. After you enroll, continue submitting a FAFSA annually to receive financial aid for the next school year.

You can also use good online calculators, like the college calculator from Northwestern Mutual that answers the question: "What will it take to save for a college education?"

This simple, easy-to-use calculator gives you quick forecasts about future college costs by letting you run different "what if" scenarios based on several variables. For instance, you can input different expectations for annual inflation; you can enter various amounts for savings you can set aside for college monthly; and you can adjust the number of college years you want to fund, and the number of years you have until your child enrolls in a college or university.

Once you input your figures, in less than five seconds, the calculator spits out your results. It tells you where colleges costs will be in a set number of years, what the total costs of college should be, as well as how much you'll need to have saved to fund college for the number of years you've selected.

What's also neat about this calculator is that if you will face a savings shortfall, three recommendations will be offered telling you how to reach your goal — either by stashing away an upfront lump sum, increasing the amount of money you save year after year, or earning a higher rate of return on your money.

Impose a Cap On Spending For College – and Stick to It

Once your child goes off to college, it's very easy to lose track of money spent on higher education. You can write a check here or there for living expenses, allow your child to take money out of your account, pay his or her credit card, and send in tuition payments to school — and before you know it you have spent many thousands of dollars. Sit down and talk with your son or daughter and set a budget. Explain what is financially feasible and possible and what is not.

Ed Fulbright, the CPA in North Carolina, urges parents: "Tell kids by their freshman or sophomore year of high school what you have available in savings and what's realistic for you to pay. Sometimes I see that kids are thinking that you've got some magical slush fund waiting for them when they turn 18 years old and that you're somehow going to pay all their bills."

When parents are upfront with their children "that will help students to set realistic goals," Fulbright says.

For those willing to borrow, it's also necessary to set limits. If all you can afford to give (or take out in loans) is, say $5,000 or $10,000 a year, then put that number on the table as your borrowing cap, then stick to it. For some advice on how much debt you can realistically manage, go to a financial planner who specializes in college financing. You can get a referral from the National Institute of Certified College Planners. Alternatively, use any number of college financing calculators that are available online, such as the one at FinAid.

Parents: Don't Skip Your Retirement Savings

Experts from the National Institute of Certified College Planners agree with me that you shouldn't sacrifice your retirement or borrow money for your child's education. Think about it this way: Little Johnny might be able to borrow for college, but who's going to loan you money for your retirement?

Allow Your Child to Borrow First

This is a more cost-effective way to take on college debt since federal Stafford Loans stand at a maximum interest rate of 6.8% for students, but PLUS loans, or Parent Loans for University Students, which are made to parents, carry an 7.9% interest rate. (An in-depth look at college financial aid policies and student loan issues are beyond the scope of this book. These topics are covered in the flagship book in this series, *College Secrets: How to Save Money, Cut College Costs and Graduate Debt Free*).

Use Online College Saver Programs Like Upromise.com and Raise.me

When you enroll in a program like Upromise, a small portion of the money you spend on everyday things — like gas for your car, clothes purchases or entertainment — gets funneled into a savings account for your child. Heck, if you were going to spend the money anyway, you might as well get a little rebate for that spending, which can help pay down future college expenses.

Raise.me is a different type of online platform that allows students, starting in 9th grade, to earn "micro-scholarships" for positive school and community behaviors. For example, students can get money for everything from getting good grades and performing volunteer work to taking the PSAT and even playing sports. Various awards are earned, little by little, based on a student's personal strengths, goals and interest. Extra-curricular activities count too, such as performing in a school play or having a role in student council. Students get credit for their efforts the instant they complete a challenge; no essay or applications required. By the time a high school student is ready for college, he or she simply cashes in all the funds that have accrued through Raise.me. As previously mentioned, schools like Cedar Crest College even grant students scholarships via Raise.me. Other collegiate partners with Raise.me include: Marist College, Rensselaer Polytechnic Institute, Tulane University, University of Dayton, and the University of Rochester, to name a few.

All parents understandably want a better life for their children, both in terms of their personal happiness and their financial security. Following the steps I've outlined above will go a long way toward helping you and your kids achieve financial stability.

* * *

A Simple Explanation of 529 Plans

Let's talk a little more now about 529 Plans, which are state-sponsored college savings programs. In my opinion, these are hands-down the single best way to save for a college education.

Here's how a 529 plan works. You (a parent or another donor) put money into the 529 plan, and it's invested in mutual funds. Professional investment advisers who are selected by the state manage the mutual funds. A 529 plan is offered by every state in the country, and you can pick any one; it doesn't have to be a 529 plan from the state in which you live. For example, in our case, we live in New Jersey, but we picked the New York plan for our children because we think it's a very good one.

Some highlights to know:

- The money you put into a 529 plan grows tax free
- All the money comes out tax free as long as it's later used for higher education (i.e. tuition, room/board, lab fees, books, supplies, etc).
- Money in a 529 plan is portable — meaning your daughter can take it with her and use it any college in the country (it doesn't have to be a college in her state, or in the state in which the 529 plan was set up).
- Money in a 529 plan is transferable. Let's say your son decides not to go to college. (Fingers crossed, that won't happen! But assume he doesn't go for whatever reason). If you have another child, you can transfer the money in the 529 plan to her, so that she can use it for college. Even if you or your spouse decides to go back to school, you could use the money to pay for your expenses.

With a 529 plan, the money is controlled by you (the donor), and is counted (for financial aid purposes and tax purposes) as an asset in your name; your daughter is listed as the beneficiary.

This can help in three ways:

1. First of all, because you control the money, she can't just have it when she's 18 or 21 (the legal "age of majority" in most states). With some funds, like trusts, when a young person turns 18 or 21, they can essentially tell mom and dad, "I want a new car" or "I want to travel and find myself," and then proceed to blow their college savings on those things ... and there's nothing the parent can do, because legally the money belongs to the child. That's not the case with 529 plans.
2. Because the asset is in your name, that helps with student financial aid down the line, when your son or daughter does go to college. All schools look at your family's finances, and determine something called your EFC, or Expected Family Contribution. In the simplest terms, that's the amount of money they expect you/your family to put toward paying for college. (Then the school offers other aid,

like scholarships, grants, work-study and loans). In determining your EFC, many colleges will count 20% of an asset owned by a child/student in the calculation for the EFC. However, only 12% of an asset owned by the parent counts toward the EFC. Again, each school is different. But this is a general guideline.

3. Many states offer a tax break to you, as the donor, for making a 529 contribution. Same deal applies for grandparents and others who contribute. Tax benefits vary, of course, based on factors such as amount contributed, income, age, and marital status.

For more info on 529 plans, visit this website: http://www.savingforcollege.com/. Savingforcollege.com and Morningstar also provide reviews and ratings of 529 plans. And remember, if you have a child: it's never too early to start saving for college!

The Magic Savings Number

In fact, if you're a parent reading this book and you happen to have a new-born or a very young child, you should open a 529 plan right away. Even if your kid is in middle school or the early phase of high school, you can benefit from a 529 plan.

"Parents want to save, but they don't know how or where to get started," says Judy Ward, a senior financial planner at T. Rowe Price, a mutual fund company that has done some interesting research into *exactly* how much a family should sock away into a 529 plan in order to cover the full cost of college at a four-year public school for an in-state resident.

If you have a newborn, the magic number is $450. That's how much you should be saving to cover your child's future public college expenses, T. Rowe Price found.

College Secret:

If a parent with a newborn saves $450 a month in a 529 Plan, by the time the child is 18, the family will have enough funds to cover four years of tuition, fees, room and board at a public college or university.

"Precisely how much to save for college has kind of been a mystery to many parents," Ward says. "Either they save the minimums required or some randomly chosen figure, but it's mostly been a guess."

Without proper guidance, many people automatically default to the minimum investments required for 529 Plans — often as little as $25 a month — and then they find that their savings are sorely lacking, Ward adds.

To make the college saving and financing process less overwhelming, experts from T. Rowe Price suggest that families think about making a "down payment" on their kids' college education if fully funding post-secondary expenses isn't possible.

"We know that $450 a month is optimal in terms of saving for a new-born's college education. But if you can only do $200 or $300 a month, then even that can make a real dent in future costs," Ward says. The same is true for parents with older children who are already in school.

Saving and investing at lower dollar levels, and at earlier timeframes, also builds a certain amount of flexibility in to a parent's budget, Ward notes. After all, many people encounter unexpected emergencies over the years. But if parents can handle those financial surprises and still stick to a regular college savings schedule, that forced discipline will pay off by the time college tuition bills come due.

"I tell people all the time: 'You either save now or you're going to borrow later. That's what it boils down to," says Ward.

*   *   *

Now that you have some saving strategies to use, it's time to tackle the all-important question at hand: How do you pick the best college to attend?

The short answer is that you must do your homework and focus on finding a school — or really, multiple schools — that represent a good academic, personal and financial fit.

The long answer is a bit more detailed. So let's explore in greater depth what this concept of "fit" is really all about.

CHAPTER 10

THE RIGHT AND WRONG WAY TO SELECT A COLLEGE

If you read the news headlines and follow press coverage about the world of college admissions, you might be inclined to think that most students go through a meticulous, well-researched college selection process.

You might also think that the majority of students — especially those at "good" high schools — have proper guidance into what colleges would be best for them.

Sadly, none of these misconceptions are true.

The Role of Friends, The "Party" School and Cute Guys and Gals

By and large, U.S. high school students pick their colleges of choice for all the wrong reasons. Many students go to a school just because it's a local campus or near their home. Other students pick certain colleges simply because their friends or boyfriends/girlfriends are going to those particular schools. And a wide swath of students, as previously mentioned, simply choose so-called "medallion" schools based on nothing more than the school's ranking or brand name.

Here are other ill-advised reasons that students have been cited as a top consideration in selecting their chosen colleges and universities:

- It's known as a "party" school
- It has cute guys or cute girls
- It was the campus with the nicest student tour guide

- It's where their older sibling or parents went to school
- It's in a popular city
- It has a cool mascot or nice school colors
- It has a great football team

None of these reasons should guide your decision-making when it comes to something as important as picking a college. In fact, some of these reasons shouldn't be on the list at all, in terms of important factors.

But that last "criteria," in particular, makes college expert Lynn O'Shaughnessy cringe. "Every time I hear a student say they want to go to a big university because of its football team, I think, seriously? You're going to make an academic choice based on a football team — and you're not even going to be playing on it? Really?"

Even for students who are passionate about sports, and love to attend games, O'Shaughnessy points out: "You're going to attend football games during, maybe, six days or so during the school year. Snap out of it!"

O'Shaughnessy believes that *non-athlete* students often select the wrong schools — and even wind up in debt — for something as careless as focusing on a university's athletics program.

As a case in point, she cites interest in the University of Michigan, a popular choice for a lot of students from that state and elsewhere too.

"When you look at state schools like Michigan those schools are incredibly expensive," she says. "Right next door, however, is a great school — the University of Minnesota — which is a lot more reasonably priced. It's also in the Twin Cities, a nice area with lots to do. The weather is about the same in both states. But I'm convinced a lot of students won't pick Minnesota because they're not known for having good sports teams."

O'Shaughnessy's advice: "Look beyond the most obvious schools that everybody would recognize on a college sweatshirt."

* * *

The consequences of making random, poor college choices are dire: far too many students wind up at institutions that aren't a good fit for them academically, personally or financially.

In a best-case scenario, students must then muddle through life on a campus that's not to their liking. In a worst-case scenario, students flit from one major to the next, or transfer schools, both of which often delay their graduation. Some students, unable to overcome the problem of a college mismatch, simply drop out of school altogether.

Interestingly, the problem of a poor college fit impacts students of all kinds, rich and poor and everyone in between; first generation and those whose great-grandparents went to college; city dwellers and urban kids; so-so students and academic standouts and more.

Even though the problem of poor college fit is universal, there are some striking differences between those at the opposite end of the income spectrum.

In this manner, the college selection process is often a tale of two worlds.

On the one hand, wealthy students might seem better positioned to find the "best" college for them. After all, they are statistically more likely to be students with higher GPAs and test scores. So, in theory at least, they should have more college options. Well-to-do students also typically have had parents who went to college. And they tend to have greater access to a better range of support systems and educational advisors — including guidance counselors in their schools, relatives who've earned four-year degrees, and paid independent educational consultants who can offer advice.

Nevertheless, these privileged students still grapple with finding the right college fit; all too often they go to colleges and universities that don't match well with their individual needs.

The same is true for their economically disadvantaged peers, even though they approach the college search process in a far different manner than wealthy students.

Improper college selection is particularly troubling for lower-income students, though, since they're already disadvantaged in key ways. Chiefly, statistics show that low-income students are more likely than better-off students to leave school without earning a degree. This issue is compounded by an inadequate college search.

According to research from Public Agenda, "Many young Americans — and especially those who fail to get a diploma — barely go through any college selection process at all. Their options may be quite limited because they do not have the financial resources to go away to school and/or they are able to consider only those options that mesh with their job schedules and family responsibilities. In many instances, college selection is more constrained and happenstance than deliberate choice."

"Among those who did not complete college, two-thirds say they selected their school primarily for its convenient location, nearly six in ten because its schedule worked with theirs and 57% because the tuition and fees were affordable.

A third based their choice on the academic reputation of the school and only a quarter on recommendations from friends and family," researchers found. Only 33% of those students considered the academic reputations of their campuses as a major reason why they chose a given school.

In other words, most college dropouts (66%) considered *convenience* most important, rather than *academics*, in selecting their school of choice. By contrast, among students who did graduate from college, the primary reasons they chose for selecting their schools were as follows:

- I thought going to this school would help me get a good job soon after I graduated (57%)
- The tuition and fees were affordable (56%)
- I could specialize or major in the exact subject I was interested in (54%)
- The overall academic reputation of the school (54%)

It's clear that there is a huge disparity in the factors driving the college decision process for students of different means.

College Secret:

Picking the wrong school, for the wrong reason, appears to be connected to the high college dropout rate in America.

Instead of going to the wrong school and risking a poor match — or even worse, risking a failure to graduate — all students would be far better served by taking much more time and being far more deliberate on the front end of their college search process. Here's how to do just that.

Choosing a School With the Best Academic, Personal and Financial Fit

Peter Van Buskirk is one of the nation's leading college experts. A former dean of admissions at Franklin & Marshall College, where he also oversaw financial aid and athletics, Van Buskirk now runs BestCollegeFit.com, and he counsels students and families nationwide about navigating higher education.

According to Van Buskirk, the key to finding the right college fit or the "best" college for you is to approach the process in a "student-centered way," as opposed to initially being focused on any particular college or university.

Begin by making personal and critical reflections about yourself. Van Buskirk suggests focusing on three things: who you are, why you want to go to college, and what you hope to get out of the college experience.

"I lead students through the self-discovery process," Van Buskirk says, "because I find that kids rarely step back to understand the character and personality issues that truly define them."

So Van Buskirk encourages students to ask and answer a series of questions in order to dig deep and make the college search process more about the student — and less about the institution.

Among the many questions you might ask yourself are:

What are my values?
In other words, what are the things that are most important to you as a person? Is it family, financial success, having a feeling of accomplishment, helping others, or something else altogether? There are no right or wrong answers. But the key is to know what makes you tick.

What do I do well?
In answering this question, think of your academics and outside pursuits, as well as areas where you may have "soft skills" such as listening to others, demonstrating compassion, time-management skills, flexibility/adaptability, or the ability to work well in groups.

What do I have to offer?
"Think not just academically or intellectually, but as someone with a range of talents, interests and perspectives," Van Buskirk says.

What do I hope to have accomplished by the time I finish my studies?
Attending college isn't just about getting A's or earning a diploma by going to class everyday, taking exams, and banging out papers. What *else* do you hope to gain out of college life? Do you want to have completed your own research into why online bullying is becoming increasingly prevalent in the U.S., or what causes nations go to war? Are you interested in using higher education as a pathway to understanding other cultures, perhaps through study abroad programs or other initiatives? Or are you interested in doing hands-on training, participating in social projects or landing paid internships? Whatever the case, think through — and even write down — what your goals are for those four years you'll be earning a degree.

Once you have a solid understanding of yourself, and your personal interests, Van Buskirk says you can identify a college with a good "fit" when it meets five crucial criteria:

1. The school offers programs of study to match your interests and needs
2. The institution provides styles of instruction to match the way you like to learn
3. It provides levels of academic rigor to match your aptitude and preparation
4. It has communities that feel like home to you
5. It values you for what you do well and what you have to offer

It's that last piece — about a school "valuing" you — that will signal whether a school is a good "financial fit." But before we discuss that aspect of fit, let's focus on the other critical elements of "fit."

Assessing a School's Programs of Study

It may sound obvious that you should select a school with programs of study that coincide with your interests, but a shocking number of students fail to consider this all-important criteria. For instance, nearly three million students begin college each year in America. While many of them declare a major, many also do not. Being undeclared is not a problem, especially since it gives you the freedom to explore various avenues of study and to learn about a range of topics. It's also important to note that not every 18-year-old is certain about his or her intended career path. That's fine, too.

However, too many students who pick the wrong schools — including both "declared" and "undeclared" pupils — later complain that what they ultimately were interested in majoring in wasn't available at their undergraduate institution.

To make sure you don't miss the mark this way, ask yourself:

Does the school offer the major you'd like to study or that you most likely want to pursue?

Does the campus have the curriculum to support your other intellectual interests?

Are special areas of interest to you already present and plentiful at the campus?

If you aren't sure what you want to study, but you do have two or three options in mind, consider this:

Are all the academic options/majors you're considering available at your chosen campus in case you wind up leaning one way or another?

Examining an Institution's Styles of Instruction

One reason many educators advocate that undergraduates get a liberal arts education is that it provides for the type of broad inquiry into a range of topics that students might not otherwise get on their own outside of college life. Where else, besides college, can a young adult delve into areas as varied as philosophy, the arts, history and comparative literature — all in the same week, or even the same day?

But teaching methodologies vary across schools, so it's not enough to know that a college or university might offer you access to a broad or "core" curriculum. You should also consider how that curriculum is delivered.

Some schools emphasize classroom time, lectures from faculty, or group projects and presentations. Other campuses focus on experiential learning, where students are often outside the classroom engaged in active, hands-on learning. Still other schools go heavy on digital learning and online classes are the norm.

Again, there's no single best way to impart knowledge to all students. So you have to know your own learning style and what suits you best.

Do you prefer in-class learning or out-of-class educational experiences best?

Does listening to lecture series by a variety of experts inspire you or bore you?

Are you most content unearthing knowledge by poring through stacks of library books — or would you prefer to learn through trial and error or your own discovery process?

For those interested in experiential learning opportunities, a school that gives you access to ample internships, plenty of field research and hands-on activities would be a good fit.

All of these are important considerations and should drive your school selections. The goal, naturally, is to find a college or university that will teach you want you want to learn in the way that is most natural or appealing to you. That way, you will stay engaged in the learning process and remain motivated to excel.

Picking a College With Academics That Match Your Aptitude and Preparation

Selecting the wrong college can lead to academic frustration for students who aim too high or too low. Many people suggest that students challenge themselves by shooting for "reach" schools, where most of the student body has achieved grades and test scores that match or exceed the applicants'. In this way, advocates say, students will have to "raise the bar" and perform at higher academic levels.

However, others say that students are simply setting themselves up for failure and heartache when they try too hard to fit into a more rigorous academic institution than they're prepared to handle. The thinking is that under these circumstances, ill-prepared students will struggle to keep up with "smarter" or better-prepared classmates students, leading to academic setbacks, such as poor grades or failed classes, as well as feelings of inadequacy and self-doubt.

Another problem on the opposite side of the coin is the college student who "under-matches" and finds him or herself at an institution that isn't intellectually challenging enough.

The solution to all these problems is for students to be realistic about their academic preparedness, and how they compare to a broad swath of peers.

To better understand whether a college or university is a good academic fit, here are some additional questions to consider:

How do your grades stack up against the incoming class of students most recently admitted to the college or university?

How do your test scores compare to the school's admitted students?

"I don't like standardized testing," Van Buskirk. "But I think that testing can be helpful to consumers in forecasting where their best fit might be."

You want to see that your grades and tests cores are in the ballpark of recently accepted students. Colleges typically report the academics for their "middle 50%" — meaning those students whose grades and test scores fall in the 25th quartile to the 75th quartile among accepted students.

If your grades fall within this range, that doesn't mean you're a shoe in. Far from it.

Having the academic profile that matches a school's typical cohort only means that "You've put yourself on the playing field and you can compete," says Van Buskirk.

To give yourself a true admissions edge, you need to be in the top 25% of accepted students. For highly selective institutions, most accepted students fall into the top 10% of those vying for admission. Among those schools, the admissions process is often far more competitive than students think, notes Van Buskirk, who is also the author of *Winning the College Admission Game* and *Prepare, Compete, Win! The Ultimate College Planning Workbook for Students.*

Remember a few other pointers too.

Even if your grades or test scores are lower than the midpoint of a school's reported ranges, that doesn't mean you won't be attractive to a campus for other reasons.

Most colleges don't have strict cutoffs, in terms of GPAs and test scores.

College Secret:

College officials often take a "holistic" approach to admissions. They consider a student's entire background and application, and say there is no minimum requirement for grades or test scores.

So don't make the mistake of misinterpreting an "average" or mean score as the minimum requirement set by any school.

Viewing a School's Communities

Lots of colleges and universities aspire to build rich, diverse communities where students of all backgrounds can thrive and grow. But each campus has its own unique culture and flavor, and what might be suitable to others — including some of your own relatives — may not seem right to you.

So ask yourself:

Does the campus feel comfortable to you?

Can you see yourself fitting in somewhere?

What kind of social environment do you prefer?

If you value diversity and inclusiveness, is that evident in the student body and faculty?

Be honest with yourself about your likes and dislikes. Some students may prefer a school with a religious philosophy, so they might favor Christian, Catholic or Jesuit institutions. Others may go in the opposite direction, preferring a college or university with no religious affiliation.

Whatever your personal preferences, it's important to find a place that you'll be happy to call your home for at least four years.

Once you've asked yourself these questions and answered them, you may find that certain schools tick off all the boxes, so to speak. Even if no campus immediately jumps out at you, over time the right ones will emerge as you continue the selection process, learn about new and different schools, and embark on college tours and visits.

Van Buskirk says that when it's time to apply to college, those who are most successful aren't just those who are most academically prepared.

"Colleges want to see how students recognize the synergies between what the campus has to offer and what the student wants to experience," he says.

Until you've visited a campus in person, Van Buskirk adds, "it's really hard to make an argument about synergies."

For those who can't afford in-person visits, one alternative that Van Buskirk recommends is getting to know the regional recruiter in your area who represents your college of choice. "That's not a perfect replacement for a campus visit in terms of understanding synergies," Van Buskirk says. "But that individual can answer many questions you may have about the institution, and if you develop a relationship, that admissions officer can later be a strong advocate for you in the admissions process."

Choosing the College With the Best Financial Fit

There is a final way to evaluate "fit," and it boils down to money.

Simply put, a school that values you will recognize that there is compatibility between you and the institution, and it will *demonstrate* its commitment to you financially — as a way to invest in your talents, interests and perspectives.

Unfortunately, most students don't get this aspect of the equation. Some think that if the school granted them admission, that's good enough, or that admission alone shows the school's interest.

I strongly disagree.

I believe that if you look hard enough, and open your mind to an array of possibilities, you can find many schools that will meet *all* of your academic and personal needs — including your financial needs — when it comes to earning a college degree.

Putting this concept into practice is sometimes a bit tricky for students and families because it means you must find those campuses that intersect in terms of being a good academic and personal fit, *in addition* to being a good financial fit.

"What might be valued with a scholarship at one school night not be valued even for admission at another school," Van Buskirk notes.

When it comes to getting into schools and winning aid for higher education, "students often see themselves as having worked hard and being deserving of an outcome. But they don't realize that they need to compete — for admissions and for aid," Van Buskirk notes.

The two primary ways to secure financial assistance from the college of your choice is to be in the top part of the talent pool at your chosen institution, and to understand the college aid process.

All two-year and four-year schools give out two forms of college aid: need-based aid based on your economic circumstances, or merit-based aid based on your talents and accomplishments. Many schools give out both. But some schools only provide need-based aid. This is true of Ivy League schools and many top private institutions.

"One of the things that some families are surprised by is that we don't offer any merit scholarships," says Tufts University associate director of admissions Karen Richardson. "As a university, all of the funding that we have goes for need-based financial aid, and we meet 100% of financial need."

College Secret:

Ivy League schools and certain top colleges and universities do provide generous *need-based* financial aid, but do not offer *merit-based* scholarships.

If money is a big consideration — and it is for most families — you absolutely *must* do some research around two crucial questions:

- *How much need-based aid are you likely to qualify for, given your family income and assets?*
- *Which colleges or universities offer merit aid for which you are likely to qualify?*

By answering these two questions, you'll develop a potential list of schools that can be strong financial fits. To find schools that offer merit aid, one terrific resource is MeritAid.com, which lets you search by college name to find merit scholarships from thousands of higher education institutions.

In addition to providing financial aid to meet your economic need or merit aid that recognizes your talents with scholarships or special academic opportunities (like study abroad, internships, research, honors programs, or special mentoring), there are other ways that schools demonstrate that they value you.

According to Van Buskirk, how a college interacts with you during the recruitment process is often a telltale sign of the way it will treat you once you enroll as a student. Specifically, colleges that value you for what you have to offer will:

- Give you personal attention throughout the recruitment process;
- Be open to answering your questions about housing, registration, or payment plans in a timely manner;
- Encourage you to explore all your college options, including "unofficial" sources of information, such as by talking with current students or alumni

Do take caution, however, in getting information from certain sources that may not have direct knowledge about a campus or the skills to guide you in finding the best financial fit. Unfortunately, this warning even includes guidance counselors in many high schools.

"It's hard enough when you have a student whose parents went to college; in most cases they don't even understand this stuff," says O'Shaughnessy. "But it's incredibly hard and even more difficult for students whose parents didn't go to college. They usually just turn to their school counselor and high school counselors are usually of no help at all regarding money matters."

"Their answer to all of this is to hold a financial aid night in the fall for high school seniors," she says. "But that's just way late in the game, and there's so much more to all of this than filing out a financial aid form."

In fairness to counselors, O'Shaughnessy says: "They know usually next to nothing about how to finance a college degree simply because they're not trained in this area. They may have Master's degrees in counseling. But those degrees don't include college planning," she notes. "It's a national scandal."

And what about using college rankings as a way to find the best college fit?

Van Buskirk and others offer this advice: Don't obsess over rankings. If you use them at all, simply let them serve as a guide or a starting point. Then supplement the rankings with your own research, college visits, feedback from students and faculty, and even your gut instincts about how you'd like to experience life on a particular campus.

As a final point of consideration, spend some time thinking about whether you'd be best served studying at a true *college* versus a university.

If you attend a college that emphasizes a liberal arts curriculum, you will gain broad exposure to a variety of disciplines, yet still have the flexibility to concentrate on a specific major. For instance, you might be a history major who also takes statistics, art and biology courses. The goal of a liberal arts education is to promote intellectual curiosity and boost your ability to think critically about a wide range of varying subjects.

By contrast, most large universities are research-focused. Many also offer pre-professional programs, such as business or law, to prepare you for advanced studies in those fields or specialized career paths. Both colleges and universities can provide experiential learning experiences, such as internships and research opportunities. But many people like O'Shaughnessy think that liberal arts colleges programs generally offer closer contact with faculty, more mentoring opportunities, smaller class size and more individualized instruction.

If you follow all of these tips, you'll find the best college for you — one where you can be happy, and one you can afford.

CHAPTER 11

GETTING IN TO YOUR "DREAM" SCHOOL

I have a question that no one has probably asked you until now: Will your dream school turn into your worst financial nightmare?

Don't think that I'm being overly dramatic. I'm completely serious!

Wouldn't it be a nightmare if you got into your so-called "dream" institution and then wound up with a ton of student loan debt that later made it nearly impossible for you to buy a home, work in your chosen field, or even get married down the road?

Or what if supposed "dream" school didn't give you much aid, and your college bills were so enormous that you had to work all the time and wound up dropping out of school due to poor grades or a lack of funds?

Unfortunately, these are all-too-common scenarios.

Americans have a collective $1.2 trillion in student loan debt and the average college grad has nearly $30,000 in student loan bills. Those who have gone on to graduate or professional schools — like law school or medical school — may have six-figure student loan debt.

I've heard many teenagers eager to attend their "dream" schools say that they "don't care" if they have to take out massive student loans to pay for their education. They say they'll figure out how to pay off those debts later. Besides, they note, paying for education is an investment in one's future.

They may be right about the investment concept, but they fail to consider a key part of smart investing: making sure you get an adequate *return* on investment. For students from a handful of schools who emerge without debt, a four-year degree does, indeed, provide a good long-term return on their investment. But that's not the case for those burdened by excessive levels of college debt. And it's not the case for the vast majority of colleges and universities in America.

Former U.S. Education Secretary William Bennett has suggested that college should be viewed as a long-term purchase, and that students should be able to generate a return on their investment in the form of their future earnings potential. Shockingly, though, Bennett's found — after looking at average costs, debt loads and lifelong earnings — that most U.S. schools fail miserably when it comes to ROI.

In fact, Bennett concluded that just 150 of America's 3,500+ colleges and universities (including for-profit and non-profit schools, as well as on-line institutions) provided positive returns. So the broad idea of college as a "good investment" simply doesn't hold water if it means students have to take on exorbitant amounts of debt for their degrees.

Sadly, the teenagers who are oh-so-willing to take on incredible amounts of loans (or ask their parents to do so) also have a huge lack of knowledge about the enormous impact of debt on one's life. They have an even bigger lack of experience in how to juggle bills, particularly large financial obligations. If you add a tough job market into the mix, which is a common occurrence for recent college graduates, a hefty student loan burden could truly become a financial nightmare.

Like excessive debt of all kind, large student loan debt takes a toll in many ways, not the least of which is the financial impact. It also affects one's health, job and career prospects, and even a person's dating or marriage prospects. These days, many cash-strapped student loan borrowers complain abut the stress of being in debt, as well as the ways their loans have dictated their job options. For example, with big student loans, lots of students can't take the jobs they *want* — especially in areas like the arts or public service fields — because they have to take jobs they *need* (i.e. higher paying jobs in areas of less personal interest). They do this out of necessity to pay off their student loans.

It's also true that a lot of people don't want to make a lifetime commitment to someone with gigantic student loans. In fact, I once wrote an article called *Student Loan Horror Stories: What's the Worst That Can Happen?* In that piece, I profiled a woman who was engaged to a fiancé that she loved very much. But when she revealed to him her six-figure student loan debt, he broke off the engagement.

So trust me when I say that at 17 or 18 years of age, young people who say they want to go to a "dream" school at any cost are simply ill equipped to fully understand the long-term implications of that decision.

Even if they're willing to pay the price, so to speak, for this choice, I believe it's up to parents to serve as the clear-thinking adults and voice their opinions about picking colleges that are affordable for a family — even if it means disappointing the student in the short run. In the long run, countless students have wound up happier (and debt free!) when their families made wise choices — that is, by picking the "best fit" school on an academic, personal and financial basis, and not based on the perceived prestige of an institution.

Jaclyn Vargo, a Harvard alumna who also received her law degree from Fordham Law School says: "The more loans you have, the more it's like being in a financial prison. The best asset you can give to yourself is to have minimal student loans. Go to an affordable school and do really, really well there."

So regardless of the campus you choose, how are you going to get into that "dream" school? Before I give you some pointers on the admissions process, let's address the very notion of having a single "dream" school.

Can We Just Stop the Madness – Or At Least Watch Our Language?

Some adults, enlightened by the college selection and admission process, say that parents should refer to their kid's top selection as his or her "first choice" school, rather than using the term "dream school."

The first time I heard this concept it immediately resonated with me. So I think it's a philosophy worth sharing.

After all, if your child doesn't get in to his or her so-called "dream" school, what message are we sending our youth? Does that rejection signal to the student that his or her "dreams" are forever dashed and will never come true? Of course that's not the case.

So students and parents: think carefully about your word choice in your conversations with one another and others.

If you must keep this phrase in your vocabulary, try not to use the singular term "dream school." Instead, use the plural phrase "dream schools."

That will be a constant reminder to everyone involved that there are many, many excellent and "dreamy" schools out there. Words have power. So being conscientious of your language will also help students maintain a healthy perspective, and keep them from becoming hyper-focused in pursuit of just *one* college or university.

An Enlighted Approach: Being Accepted at Your First-Choice School

With all that said, let's examine each aspect of your admissions application to determine how to best position yourself to the colleges of your choice. Many students want to know which part of the application a college or university considers most important. School officials often say that everything is important, because many institutions look at you in a holistic way, meaning they consider your entire application packet in context.

This is certainly true — especially for highly selective colleges — but it's also true that there is one area of your application that is usually of utmost significance: it's your academic track record.

The Most Crucial Elements: Grades and Test Scores

Specifically, grades and the rigor of a student's classes factor far more heavily into admissions decisions than do other factors, such as standardized test scores or high school class rank, data from the National Association for College Admission Counseling show.

The NACAC says that overall, colleges view the following four things — in order of importance in the admission decision: grades in college prep course, strength of curriculum, admission test scores, and overall grade point average. Among selective colleges, that accept less than 50% of applicants, overall GPA was third in importance, ahead of standardized test scores.

Here's a closer look at what NACAC has found.

Factors having considerable importance

Factor	% Agree
Grades in college prep courses	83%
Strength of curriculum	66%
Admission test scores	59%
Grades in all courses	46%
Essay or writing sample	27%
Student's demonstrated interest	23%
Class rank	22%
Counselor recommendation	19%
Teacher recommendation	19%
Subject test scores	10%
Interview	9%
Extracurricular activities	7%
Portfolio	6%
SAT II scores	5%
State graduation exam	4%

Source: survey by NACAC

Knowing that grades do matter most, how should you go about applying to and getting into any particular school?

First, you have to know the types of schools that are available.

From the standpoint of their missions, goals and sources of funding, there are a huge variety of higher education entities: public and private schools; for profit and non-profit institutions; religious and non-religious campuses; liberal arts colleges and research universities, two-year schools and four-year institutions and more.

But for the purpose of this discussion, what I want you to focus on is *the degree of selectivity* a college may have. In other words, how challenging is it for you to get into any specific type of school. Under that context, there are:

- Open admission schools accept 100% of qualified applicants
- Less selective institutions take roughly 71% to 99% of all applicants
- Moderately selective to selective schools take 40% to 70% of applicants
- Highly selective institutions accept between 20% and 40% of all applicants
- Ultra selective colleges and universities take less than 20% of applicants

Please realize that there's no standard or universal definition of what makes a school "ultra" "highly," "moderately," or "less" selective. So these are just rough guidelines. But it's important to conceptualize this hierarchy of schools when considering your statistical chances of getting in to any college of your choice.

The Pros and Cons of Open Admission Schools

A school with an "open admissions" policy is open to any prospective student that has completed high school or earned a GED. The philosophy behind these colleges is that anyone interested in learning should have a right to a higher education. At open admissions schools, your GPA and standardized test scores typically don't count in the admissions process. In fact, they're not necessary at all to attend most colleges or universities with an open admissions philosophy, though there are exceptions to that rule.

Virtually all community colleges in America operate via open admissions. So do many four-year colleges and universities. Among the four-year schools with open admissions are:

- City University in Seattle, WA
- CUNY – College of Staten Island in Staten Island, NY
- CUNY – Medgar Evers College in Brooklyn, NY

- Granite State College in Concord, NH
- Morris College in Sumter, SC
- National University in La Jolla, CA
- Pierce College in Philadelphia, PA
- Tabor College in Hillsboro, KS
- Thomas Edison State College in Trenton, NJ
- University of Maryland University College in Adelphi, MD
- University of Texas Brownville in Brownville, TX
- Utah Valley State College in Orem, UT
- Wilmington University in New Castle, DE

Students who attend open admission schools can be those with C averages or below — or they might be A students. There is often a wide mix of academic and personal backgrounds at these schools because they are far more likely to enroll non-traditional students, such as older students, transfer applicants or people returning to college to finish a degree.

So any time you're interested in specific data points, you should check directly with your schools of interest for their most up-to-date stats on grades, academics or other info that they might disclose. You should also contact a college or university directly for its most recent admissions guidelines and requirements.

If you decide to apply to a school with open admission, first check the curriculum closely and scrutinize the graduation rates. For two-year institutions and four-year schools, you want to know how many students are graduating on time from the college or university as a whole, as well as how many are graduating on time from your intended major.

Under federal law, colleges and universities are required to disclose what's known as their "150% graduation rates." This means a two-year school must disclose how many students graduated within *three* years. Four-year campuses must divulge how many students graduated within *six* years.

Community colleges and four-year institutions can also go the extra mile, of course, and state their two-year and four-year graduation rates. But not all will do so — and this is true of *all* types of colleges and universities, not just open admissions schools — because, frankly, the numbers aren't pretty when it comes to four-year graduation figures in the U.S.

Because they aren't choosy about who they accept, academic options may be limited, and student graduation rates are typically far below the national average.

The College Board operates a service called You Can Go! that allows you to search for open admission schools by state. If you're concerned about having poor grades, some of these schools are appropriate for students with C- averages or lower, as well as those without good academic records who want to go back to school and finish up a degree.

A Look at Less Selective and Moderately Selective Colleges and Universities

From an academic rigor standpoint, all colleges that aren't classified as "open admission" can be considered "selective" to a greater or lesser degree, since these colleges don't take all students who apply. Selective schools accept a wide range of applicants, from those with solid C or C+ grades all the way through to students who are straight-A applicants with 4.0 GPAs and perfect test scores.

Remember: you'll have the most success getting into a college if you match up nicely with the academic profile of its accepted freshman class. In fact, even though grades and test scores alone don't always get you into a school, at certain colleges and universities, that's exactly how the admissions process works.

For instance, at some schools, if you meet a specific minimum grade point average or achieve certain test scores, you are *automatically* granted entrance into college.

This is the case at Ole Miss, which in 2014 had a 61% acceptance rate.

"At the University of Mississippi, we're not an open admissions school, but we're close," says dean of admissions Whitman Smith.

For instance, Mississippi students are automatically admitted if they have taken basic college prep classes in high school and earned a 2.0 GPA, and a minimum composite score of 18 on the ACT, or a combined 860 score on the Critical Reading and Math sections of the SAT.

For Mississippi applicants with a higher GPA of 2.5, those residents need only score a 16 and a 760 on the ACT and SAT, respectively. Finally, those Mississippi students who achieve a 3.2 GPA don't have to submit a standardized test score. They're automatically admitted on the strength of their grades.

A similar process is in place for students who come to Ole Miss from beyond Mississippi.

"For out of state students, the automatic admission threshold is a 2.5 GPA on the core, and a minimum ACT score of 20 or a 940 SAT," Smith notes, adding: "We do not consider the writing portion of either test."

In 2015-2016, those requirements rise to scores of 21 and 980 for the ACT and SAT. The minimums increase again in 2016-2017 for ACT and SAT scores of 22 and 1020 respectively, for out-of-state students. In the 2016-2017 school year, non-residents will also have to possess a 2.75 GPA for automatic admission.

Still, if your GPA or test scores are below the school's minimum requirements, "you can submit a supplemental application and it will be reviewed," Smith explains.

Many other state schools and public colleges throughout America operate in a way similar to Ole Miss, each with its own GPA and test-score requirements.

Some selective colleges function under a "rolling admissions" system. These colleges and universities require school transcripts, and frequently ask for standardized exams too, such as SAT or ACT results. They also span the gamut in terms of selectivity. Some accept less than half of all applicants; others may take three out for four students seeking admission.

Getting Into Highly Selective and Ultra-Selective Schools

Colleges offering admissions slots through the traditional Early Decision, Early Action and Regular Decision time frames are also considered selective institutions. (See Chapter 8 for a refresher on each of these admissions processes). Again, the relative degree of selectivity varies from campus to campus based on a school's reputation, its status as a public or private institution, its goals and other factors.

But what defines rolling admission schools is that they accept applications on an ongoing, or rolling basis until classes are full. Because they often take students past the May 1 decision date, rolling admission campuses are not usually considered as "highly selective" institutions.

At most "highly selective" and "ultra-selective" schools, officials use wait lists to manage enrollment.

Because of their reputations, very selective campuses get a disproportionate number of applicants. So if these colleges and universities don't get the yield they want — meaning not enough accepted students decided to enroll — then school officials can turn to the list of students on their waiting lists.

Using data from the National Center for Education Statistics, the higher education information website eCollegeFinder created an interesting map showing the most selective college in each state. This comprehensive list of the most selective colleges in the country was based on the number of applications schools received for the class of 2017.

The map shows that selectivity rates vary tremendously from state to state. For example, the most selective school in California was Stanford, which admitted only 6% of applicants. But acceptance rates in the three states that border California were dramatically higher. The most selective school in Arizona was Grand Canyon University, which had a 55% acceptance rate. The most selective school in Nevada was the University of Nevada in Reno, which had an 84% acceptance rate. Meanwhile, the most selective school in Oregon was Corban University, which took 32% of applicants.

The state with the single most selective campus in the nation was Pennsylvania, where the Curtis Institute of Music accepted only 5% of students vying to attend that prestigious school. Wyoming ranked as the state granting access to the highest percentage of would-be college students. In Wyoming, the most selective school in the state was the University of Wyoming in Laramie, which accepted 96% of all applicants.

eCollegeFinder's map also displays various types of schools, such as art and music institutes, large state universities, and prestigious private colleges. If you've prepared yourself for the rigors of college and you've challenged yourself, don't hesitate to apply to moderately and highly selective schools, as well as ultra selective schools too, targeting those that are the best academic, personal and financial fit.

Remember: by applying to those colleges that are a good academic fit, given your school performance and educational background, you generally increase your chances of getting a "yes" from a college or university. The same is true if you have very good to great test scores.

If you must take standardized tests, do strive for the highest possible exam scores, but don't drive yourself crazy chasing 10 or 20 points on the SAT. Your time could likely be better spent doing something else more meaningful and productive. Know also that many schools super score your SAT results, picking only the highest of scores in each area over multiple sittings. In fact, many schools have computers that are programmed to process super scoring for admissions officers; in this way they only see your highest SAT scores in each section.

Consider The Timing of Your College Applications and Your Coursework

Some students are very certain about their first-choice college, so much that they apply "Early Decision" and agree to bind themselves to a school if admitted.

As an admissions strategy, applying Early Decision definitely has benefits. At many colleges, it can statistically double or triple your odds of gaining entrance. But it's not without drawbacks. That's because when you apply Early Decision you commit yourself to a school before you even see it's financial aid package.

From the institution's perspective, Early Decision works in the school's favor by helping a college or university determine which candidates are most interested in the school and who is highly likely to accept an offer of admission.

And remember: the more students that accept a school's offer of admission, the higher the "yield" rate for that school. Schools love to boost their yield, because it is one factor that propels them in the college rankings. Be certain that colleges and universities of all kinds watch and manage the Early Decision application process very carefully.

Just remember that you shouldn't "waste" an Early Decision application on an institution that's completely a reach school for you based on grades and academic fit. That's because you can only apply to one school via Early Decision. If your academic profile makes you an "outlier" academically, it's rare that you'll be viewed as a more viable candidate simply because you've applied Early Decision into a selective school.

* * *

In terms of course selection, do make sure you take appropriate courses in math, writing and science that can prepare you for college-level work. Four years of each, as well as foreign language, will make your application more competitive. And you should take honors classes or AP courses when available.

"We know that not every high school offers AP classes, IB curriculum or honors classes," says Richardson, the associate admissions director from Tufts University. "But if they're available, we want to see that students have taken them and that they've challenged themselves with the most rigorous curriculum based on what was available at their particular school."

This doesn't mean, however, that you should fret over every possible academic choice you could make, like: 'Should I take 3 or 4 AP classes in my senior year, or will it look bad if I take an elective instead of an extra science class?' As long as you've met all of a college's core requirements, and you've shown a history of challenging yourself academically, taking or not taking one or two classes is going to neither solidify nor tank your application. Schools really do look at your entire high school transcript. So if you're in your senior year of high school, or heading there, much of your track record has been firmly established.

Avoiding Senioritis

I should mention, however, that senior year is not the time to slack off. Almost every college admissions officer can tell you an unpleasant story about the time a school rescinded and admissions offer simply because a student had an about-face during senior year. A slight decline in a class or two won't get your admission revoked, especially if those less than stellar grades come in very difficult classes. But a youth who presented as a straight A-student and then all of a sudden starts racking up C-plusses or B-minuses after being admitted to college is almost certainly going to be in for a rude awakening, barring some major, plausible and worthwhile explanation about what happened.

And yes, after graduation, you *do* have to submit your final high school grades to your intended college. So keep working hard and finish strong as you wrap up high school.

"Selective colleges want to see what you will do in the classroom when you think the pressure is off—when no one is looking," says Van Buskirk of BestCollegeFit.com.

What to Know About College Essays

After your grades and test scores, one of the most important pieces of the college admissions process, and the one that you have the most control over, is the college essay. So be sure to make this an area of your application that really sings.

Your college essays should tell admissions counselors something about you that they can't find in your academic transcripts, test scores, or elsewhere in your application.

Too many students write boring, overly safe essays, or essays that reflect only what students *think* that college admissions officers want to hear. That's a big mistake. Colleges really do want to get to know the real you. So write about something that you're passionate about, or something that allows your personality, values and interests to shine through. Don't think you have to write an essay about a life-changing experience, or that you have to take some rare and unique event and spin a tale that will wow admissions officers.

Be especially careful not to engage in volunteer work just so you can later write about that community service project.

"Don't just do something for the college application," advises Richardson. Volunteering should be something you do because you are truly passionate about those efforts. Furthermore, "if a student is going to write about their summer in Belize or the work he or she is doing in terms of community service, it's important to talk about how it's affected you, what you learned from it, and how you grew from it," Richardson adds.

Peter Johnson, Director of the Office of Undergraduate Admissions at Columbia University, told students at a recent fall Open House to be careful of the "community service" essay. "There are thousands of essays written about community service projects in Costa Rica," or someplace else, said Johnson, who's been at Columbia for over 32 years.

These essays all follow the same general theme, something like: *I did community service where I went to build a school, teach impoverished children or help the poor in some way. And in the end, the people I met helped me more than I helped them.*

"You wouldn't believe how often that theme is repeated," Johnson said.

College Secret:

Think long and hard before submitting a "community service" essay that describes your volunteer work to help the underprivileged. In many cases, these essays aren't very original or memorable.

Another common theme, he added, is the "drama essay," in which students describe family members, loved ones, or even pets who've died. A variation on this theme is when students focus their essays on some kind of tragic loss or personal misfortune. If it's truly central to who you are, and such a tale gives an admissions officer a window into your life, this type of essay can work when done well. But just be mindful of how commonplace sad tales and "drama essays" are, and how admissions committees might perceive these stories.

So what is the "best" essay topic you could choose?

"Some of the best essays are celebratory essays," Johnson revealed. But he noted that it would be a mistake to get fixated on a certain "kind" of essay. "There's no one kind of essay that gets you in, nor one kind of essay that keeps you out," he said.

As long as you talk about something relevant and important to you, that's what college officials hope to see. There is only one you in the world. If you can convey how something you're passionate about connects with something the college or university offers, or how something you've done or experienced in life has led to personal growth and maturity — and prepared you for college — then your essay will be more memorable. That will make your essay stand out from the many hundreds or many thousands of other applications and essays that admissions counselors are reading.

Essays that convey a sense of the student's true personality are also typically well received. Give the admissions committee some specific insights into who you are and what has made you that way. Are you a laid back person, a creative type, a mile-a-minute go-getter, an activist, a curious thinker, a dreamer, a rabble-rouser, an organized type-A personality, or a humorous life-of-the party type of student? All of this requires some thought and introspection, which is why it's a good idea to get an early start on your college essays and not put them off until the last minute.

You'll likely come up with a first, and then a second or third draft or more, refining your essay until you're truly happy with it.

Even though you can get help, editing or other feedback from teachers, parents and others, essays should ultimately be written by you. This way the essay will capture your unique voice.

To keep track of your college essays, try the online tool CollegeEssayOrganizer.com. It's a great way to keep everything manageable and organized.

Letters of Recommendation

Letters of recommendation add to your total application package by providing the opportunity for a high school teacher or counselor to speak about you in ways that you may not be able to speak about yourself.

You should only ask for a letter of recommendation from someone who knows you well and can speak with great enthusiasm in support of your application. This doesn't always mean that you have to have earned an A from a teacher. Perhaps you got a B in a class, but that teacher is the one who can best speak to your work ethic, your determination to learn, or the fact that you came in for extra help for four weeks in a row to get that B grade.

Recommendations should also speak to your character and your strong suits as a person. Like the essay, this letter from a teacher or counselor who knows you well, is an opportunity to tell the admissions committee something additional and relevant about you that is not reflected elsewhere on your application.

To get a really good recommendation letter, you can give your teacher or counselor an up-to-date resume or an activities worksheet as a reminder of what you've accomplished. Mostly, doing your best and developing a close relationship with your academic advisors and mentors is the way to get the strongest possible letter.

In picking a teacher to ask, the more compelling and valuable letters often come from teachers who've known you for a while and/or who've taught you in your junior or senior year. That is the time when you are likely peaking in terms of academic development, and you are making meaningful contributions both in and outside the classroom to which these teachers or counselors can attest.

Extra-curricular Activities

Having extra-curricular activities is a good way to show your college readiness, but probably not or the reasons you think.

Colleges care about your extracurricular activities mainly for two reasons. They want to know where you passion lies, and they want to know how engaged you are in aspects of life *outside* the classroom.

And above all, "don't just pack a bunch of extracurricular activities into your senior year," says Richardson. "Schools look for a commitment over time."

Taking advantage of opportunities to be involved in extracurricular pursuits at your school or in your community is important because admissions officers know your current experiences represent only a sliver of what will be available to you at a college or university campus.

Schools *want* you to come and take advantage of their resources and opportunities. And one of the best ways they can gauge if you'll do that is if you're *currently* doing it — or making the most of whatever tools, resources and opportunities present themselves to you now.

College Interviews

Most colleges in the U.S. do not require on-campus interviews. However, if you are offered the opportunity, you should take it. You'll know this is a wise move, especially if a campus says an interview is "optional" or "encouraged." In such instances, interviews are often seen as a strong signal of interest on your part, something that aids you in the admission process.

One question you should always ask a school is whether the interviews it offers are informational in nature, or evaluative. Generally speaking, large universities and colleges may offer informational interviews, which most college experts say won't really help or hurt your candidacy in any way. These informational interviews are designed to let you ask questions about a campus and let an interviewer learn more about you and your interests, and to share that feedback with the admissions committee.

On the other hand, many interviewers for smaller colleges, and liberal arts schools in particular, say that interviews can be very important for evaluation purposes. Under these circumstances, a school may determine whether you'd "fit in" on a given campus, or how you would complement the student body. Such interviews are rarely the deciding factor in whether a school chooses to admit or deny a candidate. But a really excellent interview, or a total bomb of an interview — say you fail to show up, or you spend half the time checking your smart phone — can definitely tip the scales one way or another when it comes to admissions.

College Secret:

College interviews may feel like high-stakes events. In reality, they usually don't make or break a student's chances of college acceptance.

Whatever the case, know that you should always take a college interview seriously and put your best foot forward. Realize also that interviews may be done on campus, in your local area, and often with college alumni.

Whenever interviews take place, try to be yourself and not stress about the meeting. Doing a practice interview with a parent or teacher can help calm any jitters you may have. As part of your mock interview, rehearse explaining why you see a college as a good potential fit. But don't rehearse so much that you come off sounding robotic or like you're giving canned answers. Additionally, don't drive yourself crazy with worry about the particulars of any interview, whether it's conducted in person or via a social media platform like Skype. For in-person interviews, make sure you smile and shake the person's hand when you meet to make a good first impression.

* * *

Once you make it through all of these steps, the only thing left is for you to sit back and wait for your college admissions letters to arrive. If you target the right schools, you'll no doubt have options when it comes to selecting the best possible college or university where you'll later spend four years of your undergraduate life.

Unlike other, less-informed students, because you've read *College Secrets for Teens*, you now know what it takes to get into your top choice college or university, wherever that campus may be. You also now know how to pay for pre-college expenses, prepare yourself for college, and do it all without busting the family budget.

The next phase in the process is to bone up on the financial challenges that college itself presents. Don't think for a moment that your only post-secondary expenses will involve upfront college costs, such as tuition, fees, room and board. Remember my earlier advice about paying attention to *all three areas* of college costs, including:

- *Pre-college* expenses
- *Upfront* college costs
- *Hidden* college fees

College Secrets for Teens tackles all the pre-college expenses you'll face. The flagship book in this series, *College Secrets*, will arm you with all the tools and resources you need to eliminate or reduce a slew of upfront college costs, as well as dozens of hidden costs no one tells you about. So check out *College Secrets* as you continue on your journey toward earning a four-year degree.

It's my sincere hope and prayer that you will find the best college fit for you, and that during and after your studies you will enjoy all the academic, personal and professional success you so richly deserve.

Best Wishes!

Lynnette Khalfani Cox,
The Money Coach

$\mathcal{J}$NDEX